Table of Contents

- Flowers: Rose, Cherry Blossom, Dandelion, Sunflower
- Trees: Oak, Willow, Pine, and others
- Animals: Lions, Wolves, Birds, Bears, and more
- Landscapes: Mountains, Oceans, and Forests
- Chapter Conclusion

- Triangles: Stability, Change, Spiritual Growth
- Circles: Eternity, Wholeness, Unity
- Mandalas: Spirituality, Balance, and Inner Peace
- Abstract Symbols: Freedom, Uniqueness, and Individuality
- Chapter Conclusion

- Sun: Power, Vitality, Enlightenment.
- Moon: Intuition, Femininity, Change
- Stars and Constellations: Guidance, Ambition, Dreams
- Planets: Exploration, Discovery, Beauty
- Fire: Transformation, Passion, Energy
- Water: Renewal, Emotional Depth, Adaptability
- Air: Freedom, Communication, Intelligence
- Lightning: Sudden Change, Power, Inspiration
- Comets: Rare Moments, Important Events
- Galaxies: Infinity, Exploration, The Unknown
- Chapter Conclusion

Introduction

Tattoos have been etched into human history, worn proudly on the skin as symbols of identity, milestones, and personal stories. While some tattoos are bold declarations of individuality, others carry quieter, more intimate meanings. Each design can be as unique as the person who wears it, offering glimpses into their thoughts, values, and life experiences.

Over the years, tattooing has transcended from a practice associated with specific cultures and tribes to a universal art form embraced by people of all backgrounds. Yet, despite the growing popularity of tattoos, one truth remains constant: every mark, whether minimalistic or intricate, can hold significance. For some, a tattoo is a reminder of an important life lesson, a tribute to a loved one, or a token of self-expression. For others, it may represent strength, transformation, or underlying beliefs.

In a world where imagery and symbolism are powerful forms of communication, tattoo meanings have evolved and expanded to include a vast array of interpretations. Nature, animals, abstract shapes, and even everyday objects take on a deeper importance when chosen as permanent body art. The choice of a tattoo often reflects one's inner world, capturing individual philosophies, aspirations, and even emotions in a way that resonates far beyond the visual.

What makes tattoos particularly fascinating is the diversity of meanings attached to them. A simple symbol, like a feather, can mean freedom for one person and a spiritual connection for another. A wave may speak of life's fluidity to one while it represents the incredible forces of nature and resilience to someone else.

This book explores over 100 tattoo meanings, helping you discover the stories behind popular designs and those you might not have considered before. Whether you're thinking about getting your first tattoo or adding to your existing collection, this guide aims to inspire and provide insight into the wide range of symbols available.

Choosing a tattoo is a meaningful endeavour. It's more than just selecting an image—it's about connecting with what that image represents. As you turn these pages, take the time to reflect on what each symbol could mean for you. A tattoo is, after all, a permanent commitment to a part of yourself. In this sense, the meaning behind the design can be just as important as its aesthetic.

Whether you're drawn to the powerful symbolism of a lion, the intricate beauty of a geometric pattern, or the enduring meaning of a single word, the goal is the same: to make sure your tattoo reflects who you are, where you've been, and where you want to go. Through this discovery of understanding tattoo meanings, we hope you find inspiration and clarity in selecting the right design that speaks to your unique story.

Tattooing has the remarkable ability to merge the external and internal worlds. It's a language without words—a visual expression that transcends barriers. From delicate minimalistic designs to full-body artwork, tattoos are a canvas where life memoirs, dreams, and memories can be remembered until the end. Yet, with such permanence comes the importance of thoughtful selection. The decision to mark your body with a specific image should hold meaningful interpretation, as it stays with you on your adventure through time.

For some, the appeal of a tattoo is rooted in its visual beauty, while for others, the layered meanings behind the symbol hold more substantial value. Some tattoos are worn as armor—symbols of protection or strength—while others might act as reminders of challenges faced and overcome. These visual cues become anchors in time, reminding us of who we were when we chose to be tattooed. A simple arrow could represent a sense of direction and purpose, pushing someone forward in life. A compass, on the other hand, might speak to someone who is navigating new territory—be it physically, mentally, or emotionally.

One of the most powerful aspects of tattoos is their ability to evolve with us. What may have represented one stage of life can take on new meanings as time passes. For example, a phoenix tattoo, chosen to symbolize rebirth after a problematic period, may grow to embody the wearer's continued empowerment in the face of future challenges. Tattoos, like their meanings, are never static. They move with the tides of our experiences, carrying different weights as our perspectives shift.

This book is designed to help you explore the layers of meaning, offering insights into the symbolism behind more than 100 tattoo designs. Some are deeply rooted in ancient cultures, while others are more contemporary or abstract. By diving into this wide variety, you'll discover how universal themes—such as transformation, balance, love, and strength—are expressed through diverse tattoo styles. Each section of the book is crafted to explore the deeper meanings behind familiar and lesser-known designs, helping you connect with tattoos that resonate personally. Choosing a design often involves deep introspection, whether you're leaning toward bold, statement-making tattoos or more subtle, delicate ones. This book encourages that process by providing context for various symbols and meanings. The goal is not to tell you what your tattoo should mean but to inspire and offer ideas that align with your experiences and desires. You may find that a particular symbol captures your attention immediately, or perhaps something you've never considered will spark an idea that feels just right.

As you read the pages of this book, remember that tattoo meanings are highly personal. While certain designs may have established symbolism within specific cultures or traditions, the ultimate meaning of your tattoo lies in your interpretation. You may draw from ancient meanings, modern symbolism, or something unique to your journey. It's fundamentally about what feels significant and genuine to you.

In this sense, tattoos are as much about storytelling as they are about art. Each mark on the skin is a piece of a larger narrative, one that is constantly being written and rewritten as you move through life. What you choose to carry with you in the form of a tattoo is more than a design—it's a reflection of your inner world, your past, your present, and perhaps even your future.

Whether you're already adorned with ink or considering your first design, we hope that by the end of this book, you will feel empowered to make choices that honour your individuality and tell your story in the most meaningful way possible.

Chapter 1: Nature-Inspired Tattoos

Nature has always been a profound source of inspiration for artists, particularly tattooists. The natural world's breathtaking beauty and intricate details encourage individuals to express their bond with the environment through body art. Nature-inspired tattoos capture the aesthetic essence of our surroundings and can convey strong individual meanings and moving connections. This chapter will delve into various nature-inspired tattoo designs, focusing on flowers, trees, animals, and landscapes while exploring their symbolism and implications.

Flowers

Flowers rank among the most cherished tattoo motifs, imbued with rich symbolism and meaning. Each flower's unique connotation makes them versatile options for those wishing to express specific emotions or ideals. Their adaptability allows for minimalist designs and intricate, elaborate pieces, solidifying their status as a timeless choice in tattoo art. Flower tattoos embody diverse meanings, often rooted in cultural backgrounds, personal narratives, and the inherent beauty of nature. Take, for instance, the rose—a classic symbol of love, passion, and, in some contexts, loss or sacrifice. Beyond its romantic associations, the rose's thorns add another layer of meaning, representing the duality of beauty and pain and the understanding that love often comes with difficulties. This complexity makes the rose a versatile and significant symbol for many wearers, resonating on various personal levels. As we explore the elements of nature in tattoo art, we will reveal how these symbols function as unique displays and vital connections to the vibrant planet we inhabit.

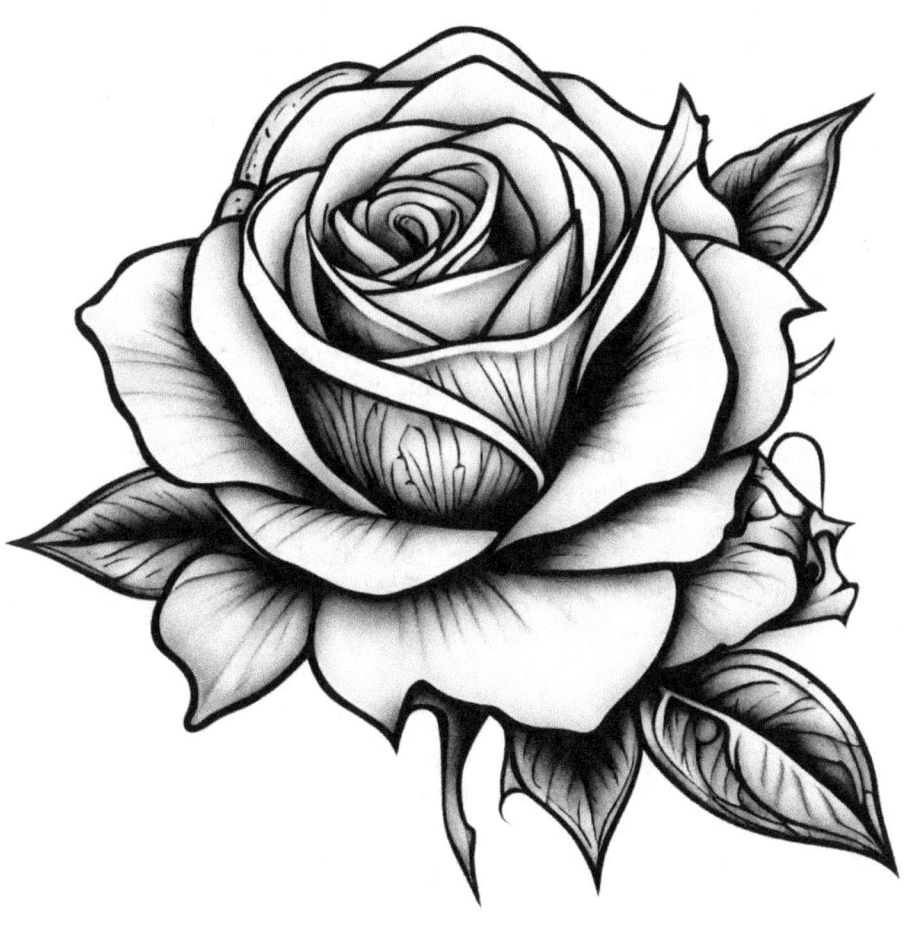

A rose tattoo design

1. Rose

Rose tattoos can be intricately detailed, capturing the flower's delicate petals and lush greenery or designed more abstractly. They are among the most popular tattoos and have been tattooed worldwide for many years. The rose is one of the most iconic flowers in tattoo art with different colors representing different meanings:

Red Roses represent romantic love and passion, often commemorating important relationships or moments.

White Roses symbolize purity and innocence, making them famous for memorial tattoos or as tributes to lost loved ones.

Yellow Roses signify friendship and joy, representing the bonds of friendship and celebration of life.

Black Roses, although less common, can symbolize death, mourning, or the end of a relationship.

2. Cherry Blossom

The cherry blossom, or sakura, symbolizes the fleeting nature of life and beauty. In Japanese culture, the cherry blossom represents the transient nature of existence, reminding us to appreciate the beauty of life while it lasts. These fleeting blossoms remind us vividly of life's impermanence, encouraging us to cherish every moment.

A cherry blossom tattoo often signifies love, renewal, and the beauty of new beginnings. It can represent a celebration of life, capturing the essence of spring and the hope it brings. Designs may feature branches laden with blossoms, often intertwined with other elements, creating a harmonious and aesthetically pleasing tattoo that evokes one to flourish and appreciate the present moment.

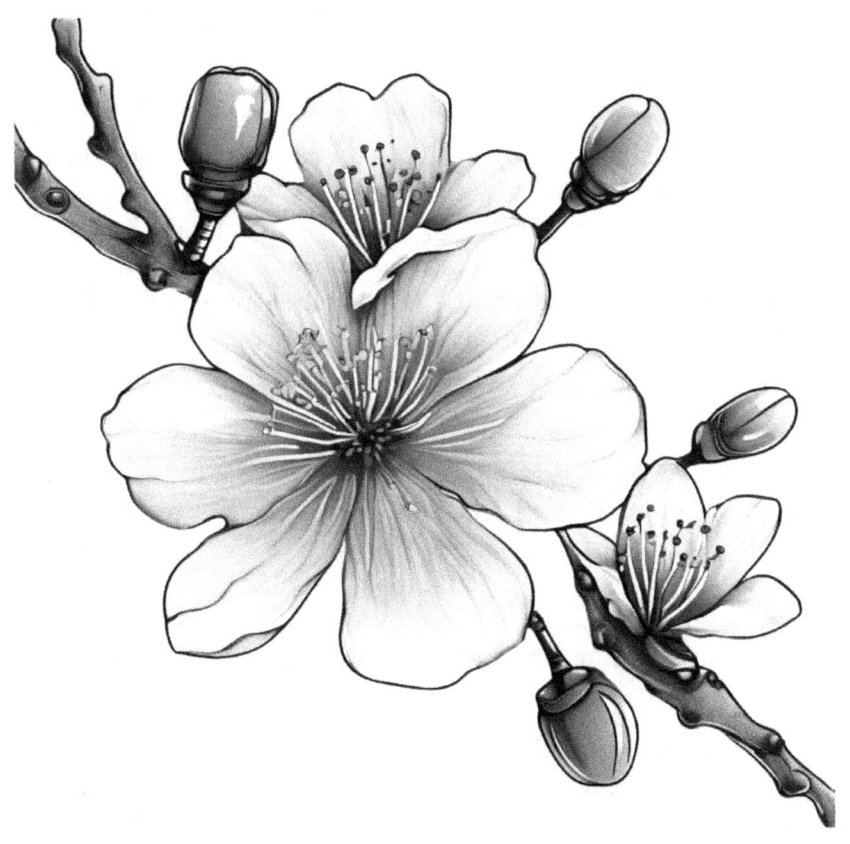

A cherry blossom tattoo design

3. Dandelion

The dandelion, often seen as a common weed, carries profound meanings, particularly in tattoo art. Dandelions symbolizes a belief of hope and the idea of wishes coming true. When the flower goes to seed, it transforms into a fluffy sphere, and blowing on the seeds is said to carry one's wishes into the universe.

A dandelion tattoo can represent life's course, embracing change and the ability to thrive hopefully in adversity. It is a gesture to remain wishful and make the best of one's circumstances. The design can be playful, capturing the whimsical nature of dandelions, often depicted with seeds drifting away in the wind, symbolizing freedom and the pursuit of dreams.

4. Sunflower

Sunflowers are bright, cheerful flowers that symbolize adoration, loyalty, and positivity. Their tendency to turn towards the sun represents the pursuit of happiness and the idea of seeking light in dark times. Sunflower tattoos often promote warmth, joy and faithfulness making them popular choices for those who wish to embody positivity.

In addition to their aesthetic appeal, sunflowers can also signify loyalty, vitality and a sense of belonging. They can be designed in various styles, from realistic depictions to more abstract representations, allowing individuals to uniquely express their connection to happiness and hope.

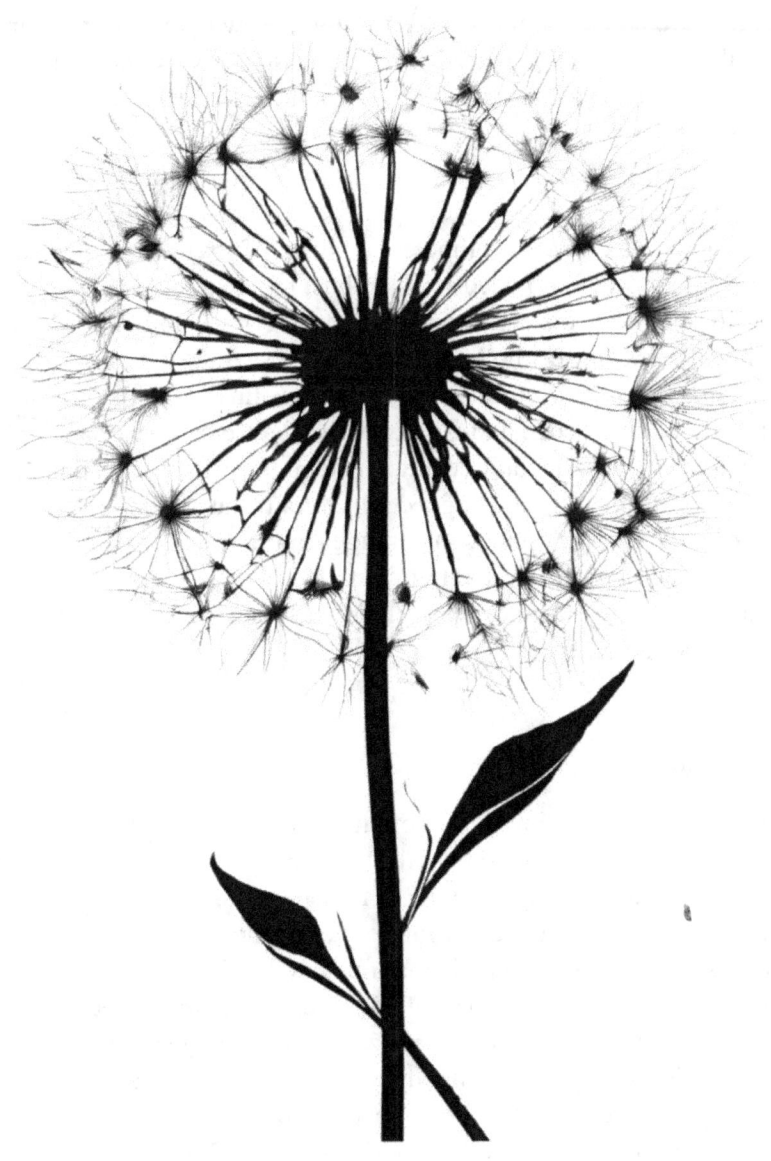

A dandelion tattoo design

Trees

Trees are potent symbols of knowledge, growth, and connection to the natural world. They can represent stability, wisdom, and the interconnectedness of life, making them trendy choices for tattoos.

1. Oak

The oak tree stands as a timeless emblem of strength, endurance, and longevity. Renowned for its robust nature and deeply anchored roots, the oak represents unwavering stability, appealing to those who hold strength and steadfastness in high regard. Across various cultures, the oak is linked to wisdom and profound knowledge and is frequently viewed as a guardian of ancient truths. An oak tree tattoo can embody many meanings, such as clarity, familial connections, or a tribute to one's heritage and roots. Design options may range from intricately detailed depictions showcasing the tree's gnarled branches and lush leaves to more abstract interpretations emphasizing its sheer size and lasting presence.

2. Willow

In contrast, the willow tree is often characterized by its flexibility, grace, and adaptability. Its long, flowing branches and delicate leaves gently swaying in the breeze can spark feelings of tranquility and peace. In various cultures, the willow is regarded as a symbol of healing and emotional well-being, making it an ideal choice for tattoos that reflect times of healing or recovery. A willow tree tattoo can symbolize the remarkable ability to bend without breaking, embodying the spirit of embracing life with poise and grace. Its design can be soft and ethereal, capturing the essence of the tree's beauty and fluidity.

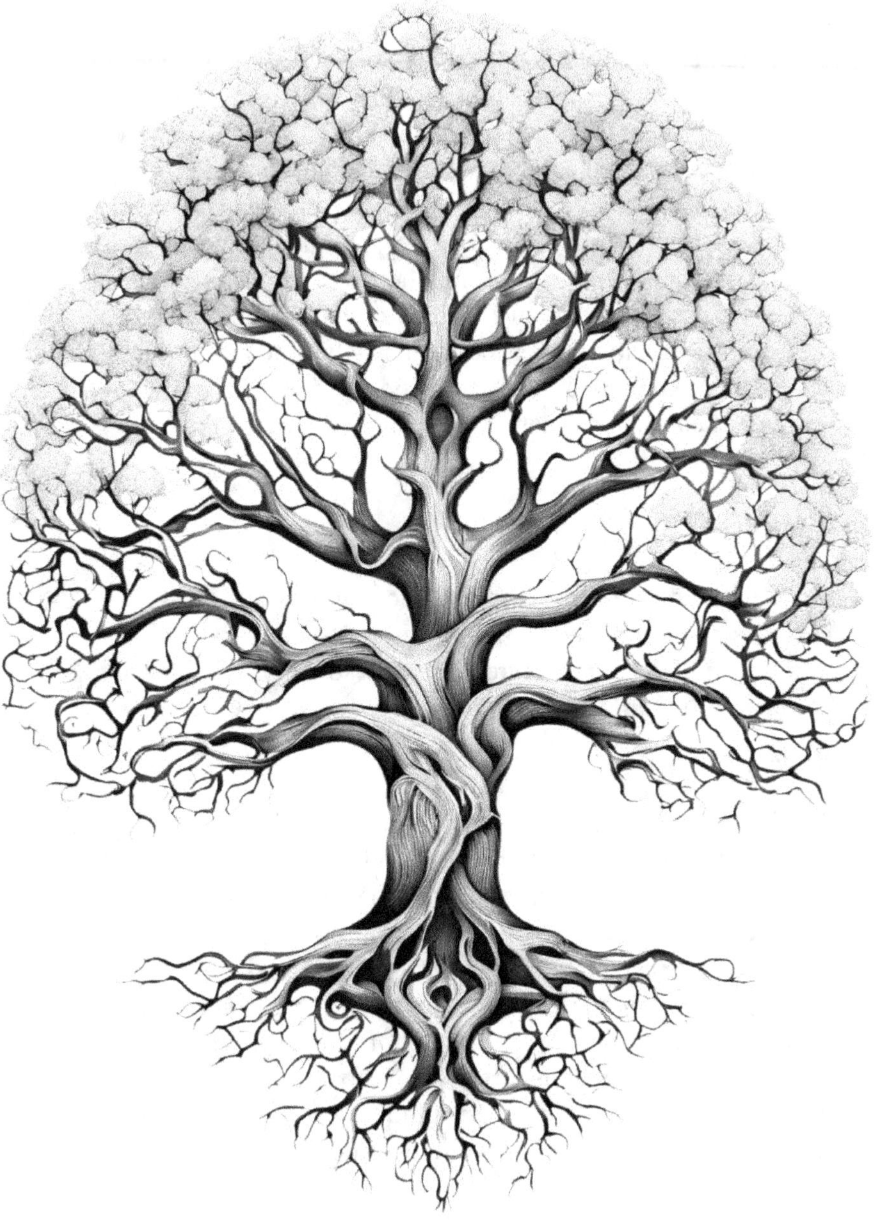

An oak tree tattoo design

3. Pine

The pine tree symbolizes endurance, longevity, and the idea of eternal life. Known for its ability to thrive in harsh conditions, the pine represents fertility and adaptability. In many cultures, the pine tree is associated with purity and clarity and is often viewed as a guardian of sacred spaces. A pine tree tattoo can embody fortitude, a long life, or a deep connection to nature. Its design can range from simple silhouettes to intricate representations of its unique needles and cones, allowing for diverse interpretations. For individuals who find comfort and inspiration in nature, a pine tree tattoo is a beautiful tribute to the enduring beauty of the natural world.

Animals

Animal tattoos are compelling symbols of instincts, emotions, and personal traits. Each animal boasts its own narrative, allowing individuals to express their personality, values, and beliefs through their chosen designs.

1. Lion

The lion is often regarded as the king of the jungle, symbolizing courage, might, and leadership. A lion tattoo represents bravery and the ability to confront dire straits head-on. It embodies the qualities of a protector and is frequently associated with nobility. In many cultures, the lion signifies authority, making it a fitting choice for those who resonate with leadership qualities. The design can vary from realistic depictions of the majestic animal to stylized interpretations, often emphasizing its mane and fierce gaze. For individuals who cherish bravery and determination, a lion tattoo is a popular choice in modern times.

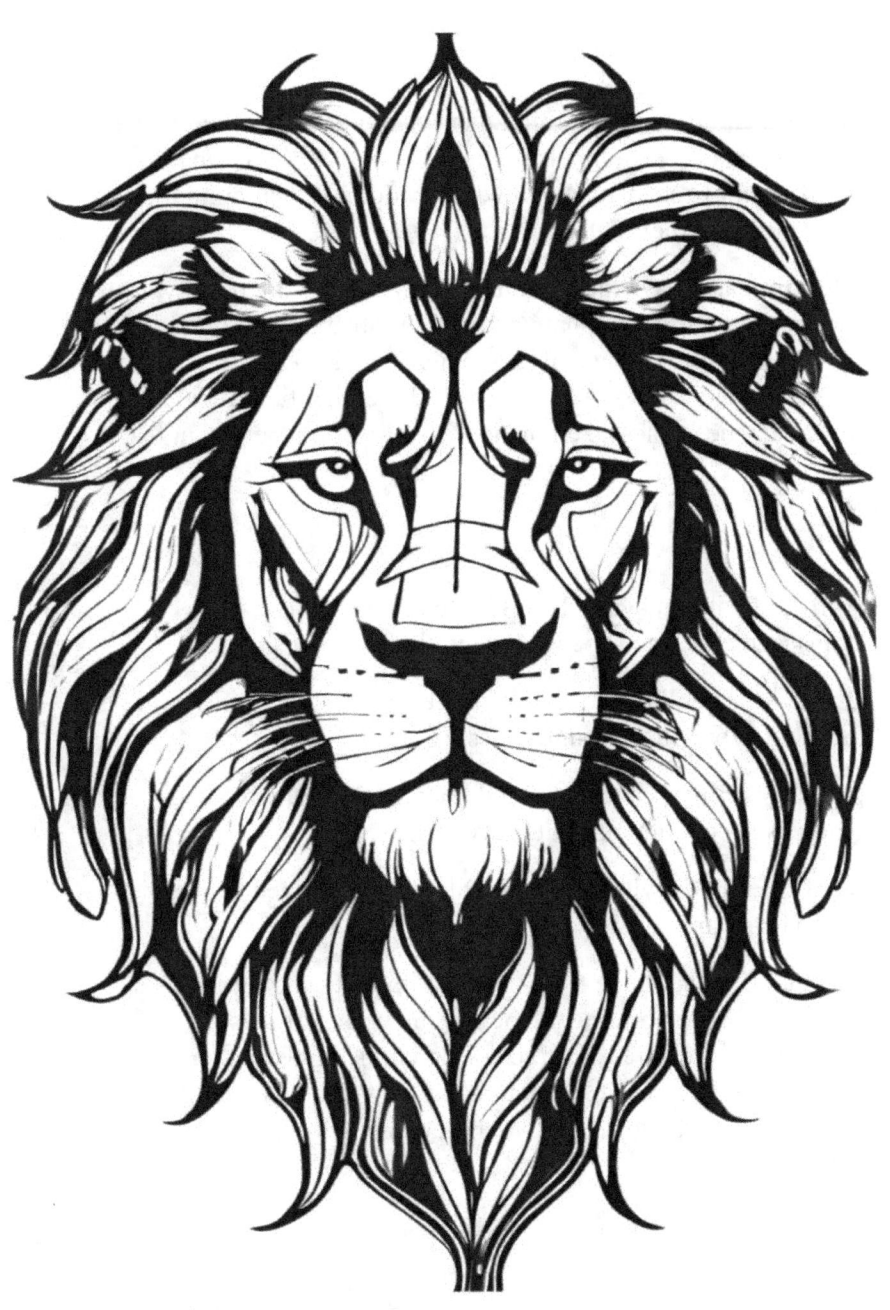

A lion tattoo design

2. Wolf

Wolves embody loyalty, intelligence, and intuition, and they are often seen as pack animals that work together. Additionally, the wolf symbolizes instinct and wild freedom, appealing to those who embrace their untamed side.

Designs can vary widely, from stunningly realistic portrayals of wolves in their natural habitats to more abstract interpretations that capture the essence of this majestic and mysterious creature. For individuals who intend to show these qualities, a wolf tattoo also becomes a classic emblem of loyalty and inner strength.

3. Bird

Birds are vibrant symbols of freedom, perspective, and transcendence, each species rich with unique meanings.

Eagles: Symbolize strength, courage, and vision, representing the ability to soar above tough times.

Doves: Signify peace, love, and hope, making them distinct choices for commemorating love or loss.

Owls: Embody wisdom and intuition, often linked to deep knowledge and mystery.

Bird tattoos can range from elegant silhouettes to intricate illustrations, celebrating the beauty and grace of these captivating creatures. For those who cherish freedom and exploration, a soaring bird tattoo can powerfully symbolize the desire to rise above and fully embrace life's wondrous adventures.

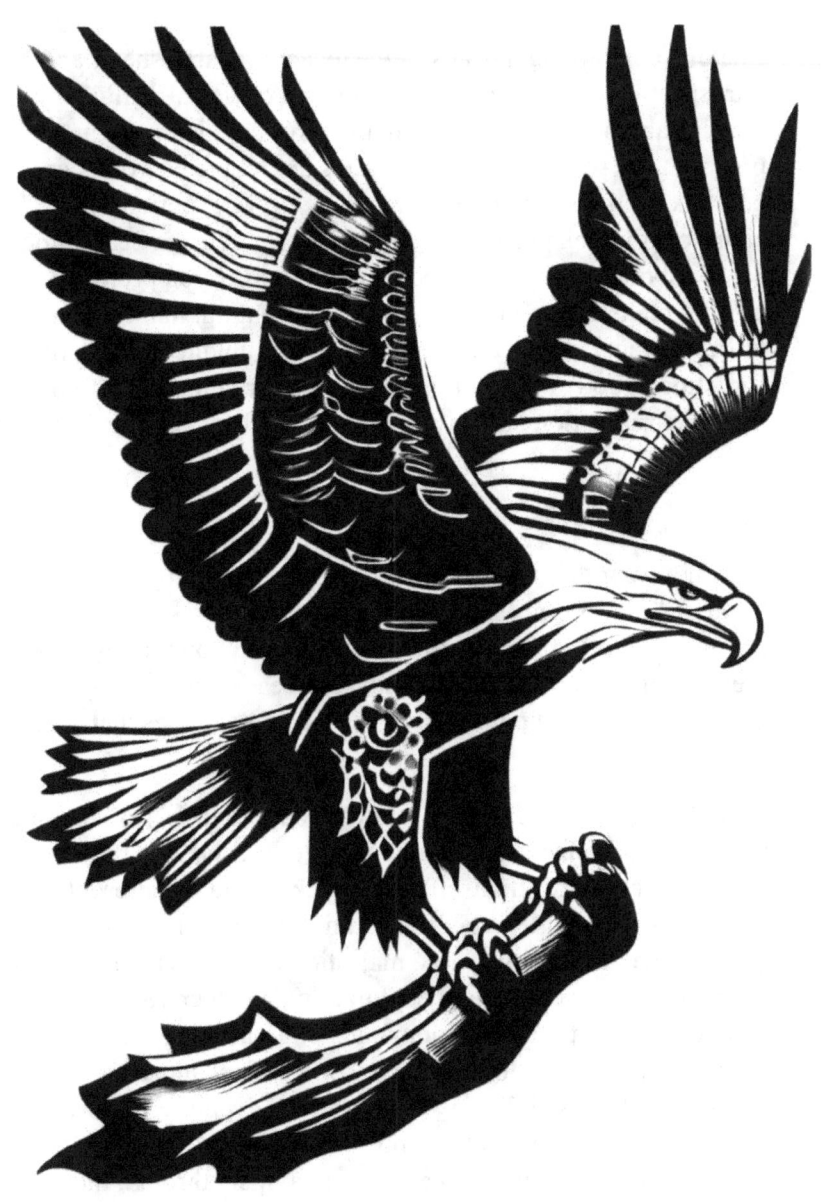

An eagle tattoo design

4. Bear Tattoos:

Imagine embodying a bear's fierce tenacity, fearlessness, and introspection daily. Bear tattoos can be a powerful reminder of bravery and protection, symbolizing physical toughness and prowess. These magnificent creatures are revered across various cultures for their immense strength. If you've experienced significant life changes and emerged more robust, a bear tattoo can symbolize that journey perfectly. Whether you prefer an artfully realistic depiction of a bear in its natural habitat or a more abstract design, a bear tattoo offers a unique opportunity for tattooed body art. Let this bold symbol remind you of your inner determination and adventurousness whenever you glance at it.

Landscape Tattoos:

Why not wear the beauty and majesty of nature on your skin? Landscape tattoos not only showcase the breathtaking scenes of the natural world but also reflect your association with it. From the towering mountains to the endless oceans, these designs promote feelings of peace, adventure, and the stories that shape your expedition.

Mountain Tattoos: Mountain tattoos are more than just beautiful art; they symbolize venturesomeness, endurance, and the incredible climb of life itself. Each peak you face represents an obstacle to overcome, and each summit you reach signifies your triumph over adversity. These majestic designs invite exploring your spirit of adventure and exploration. Whether you choose a simple outline of majestic mountains or an intricate landscape featuring lush trees, flowing rivers, or a radiant sunset, a mountain tattoo will display your love of adventure. Embrace the essence of discovery, and let your mountain tattoo be a testament to your inner adventure seeker as you navigate through the rough terrain of life. Choose a tattoo that adorns your skin and tells your story—one of bravery and an unyielding connection to the beauty of nature!

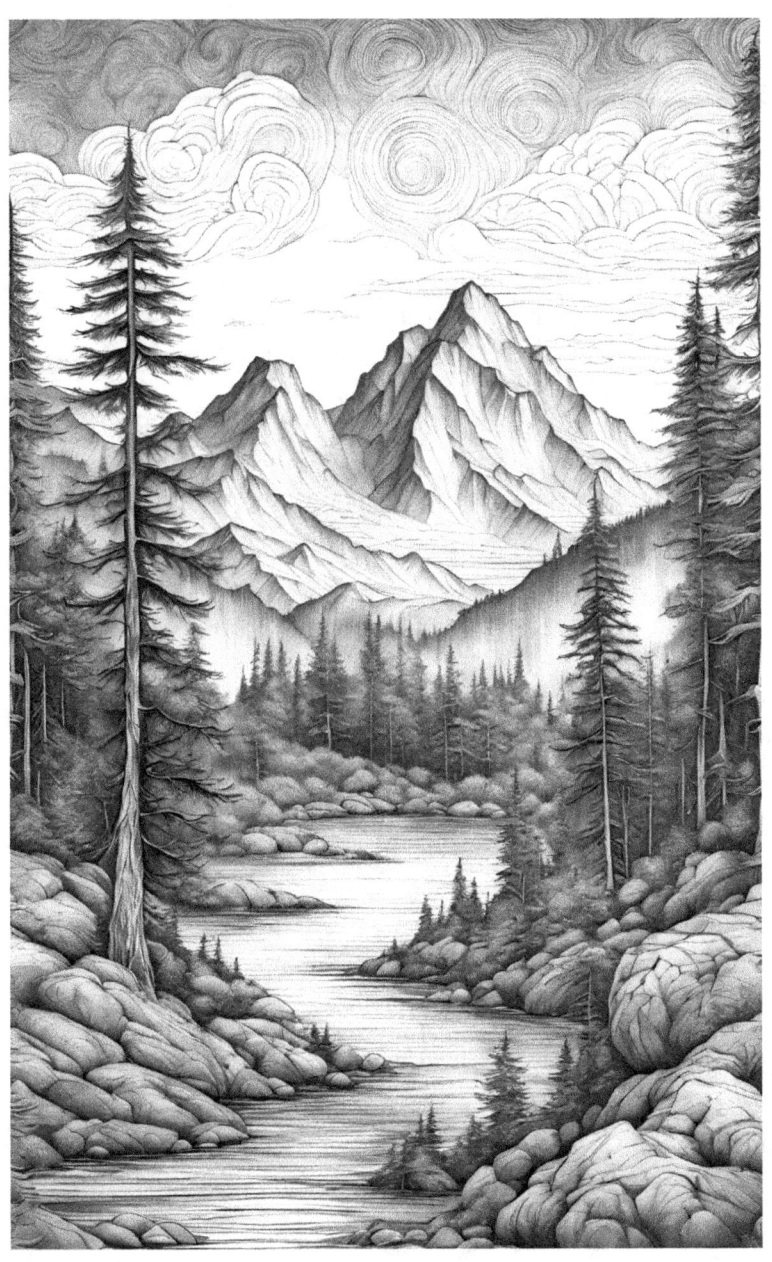

A mountainous landscape tattoo design

2. Oceans

The ocean represents vastness, depth, and the ebb and flow of life. Ocean tattoos can symbolize emotional depth, mystery, and the love of the sea. Waves are compelling and common symbol of the love an individual can have for watersports, be it sailing or skimboarding. An ocean tattoo often shows feelings of tranquility and connection to nature, beautifully capturing the power of waves crashing against the shore or the serene calm of a still sea. Designs can incorporate various elements, such as boats, seashells, or intricate marine life, allowing one to be creative with the design. For those who find peace in the ocean's vastness, an ocean tattoo is a sign of life's beauty and unpredictability, offering comfort and inspiration through its stunning imagery.

3. Forests

Forest tattoos symbolize growth, mystery, and the interconnectedness of life. They represent a sanctuary of peace and the grounding essence of nature. Forests are often associated with exploration, adventure, and discovery, inviting individuals to delve into their innermost thoughts. A forest tattoo can capture the beauty of towering trees and the intricate details of the forest floor, often incorporating elements like wildlife, leaves, or the changing seasons. Designs can vary from realistic representations to abstract interpretations, allowing individuals to express their unique connection to the natural world. For those who find solace in the forest's beauty, a forest tattoo is a stunning display of their bond with nature, instilling feelings of serenity and reflection.

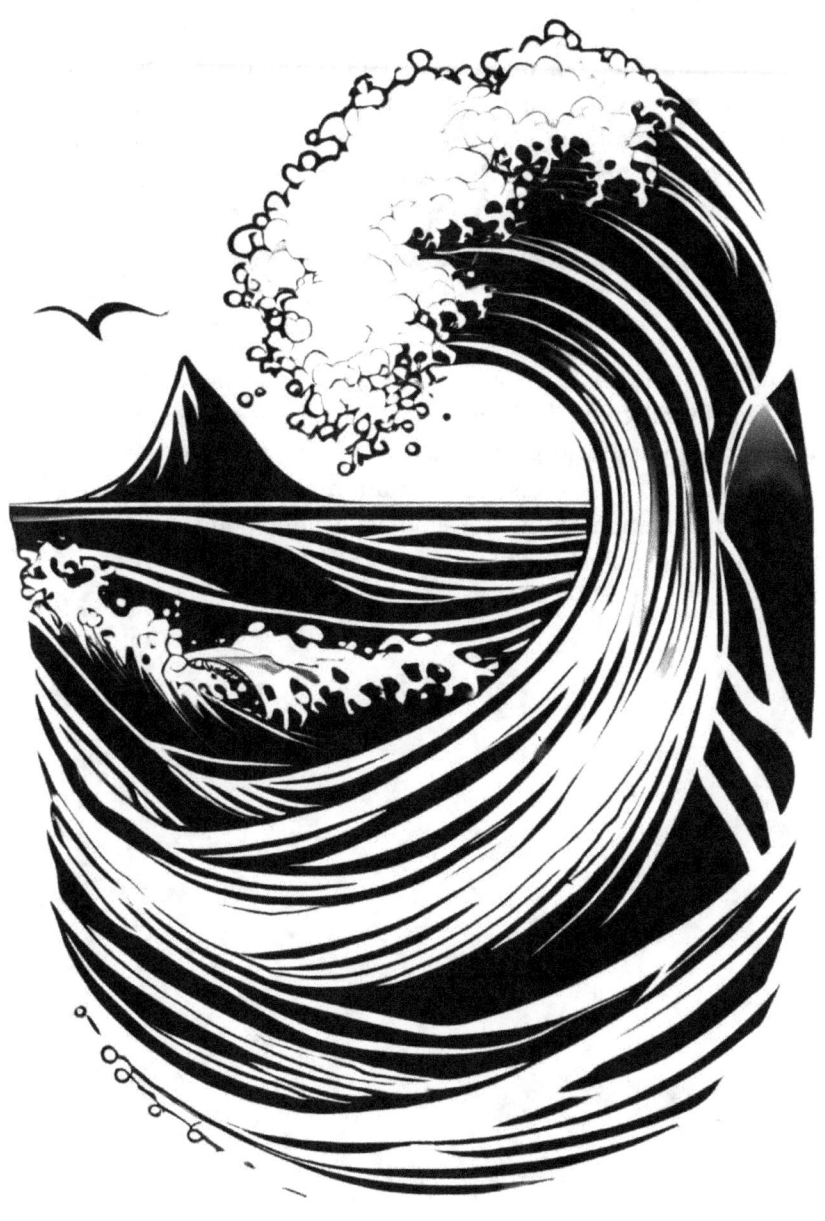

A tattoo design of the ocean

Chapter Conclusion

Nature-inspired tattoos provide a personal way to express one's connection to the natural world around us. These tattoos carry rich meanings and vibrant spirit, whether illustrated through the delicate beauty of flowers, the enduring strength of trees, the toughness of various animals, or the breathtaking majesty of diverse landscapes. Each unique design tells an intricate story, reflecting exploration, values, and aspirations while fostering a sense of identity and belonging to nature's wonders..

By choosing nature as a source of inspiration for their tattoos, individuals celebrate the beauty of the natural world and honor their personal expedition and the emotions that shape their lives. As nature continues to inspire and nurture, these tattoos provide a lasting indication of the profound connection between humanity and the environment.

Chapter 2: Geometric and Abstract Tattoos

Geometric and abstract tattoos are modern exhibits with basic shapes and intricate patterns to convey a variety of meanings. This artistic, minimalist approach renders them highly versatile and adaptable to diverse personal styles and beliefs. Each shape encapsulates unique symbolism, and even minor variations in design can introduce new layers of meaning. This chapter delves into four popular types of geometric and abstract tattoos: triangles, circles, mandalas, and abstract symbols.

Triangles: Stability, Change, Spiritual Growth

1. Stability

The triangle, one of the simplest geometric forms, boasts universal symbolism. Its three sides provide inherent stability, making it an emblem of balance and strength. Unlike other shapes, the structure of a triangle is firm and cannot be easily altered, representing permanence and a well-structured nature. In tattoo designs, triangles often signify a solid foundation in one's beliefs, principles, or relationships. Individuals who seek stability frequently choose this shape as a sign of their structuredness and the steadfastness.

Moreover, the triangle can illustrate interconnectedness. Its three points may symbolize equilibrium among different aspects of life, such as mind, body, and spirit, or past, present, and future. These symbols resonate deeply with those who aim for balance in their emotional and spiritual journeys. Additionally, variations in the triangle's design—such as incorporating colors or additional elements—can enhance its meaning. The triangle also embodies balance by connecting its points, representing harmony between mind, body, and spirit. Each vertex signifies a vital aspect of life, promoting equilibrium in our emotional and spiritual course.

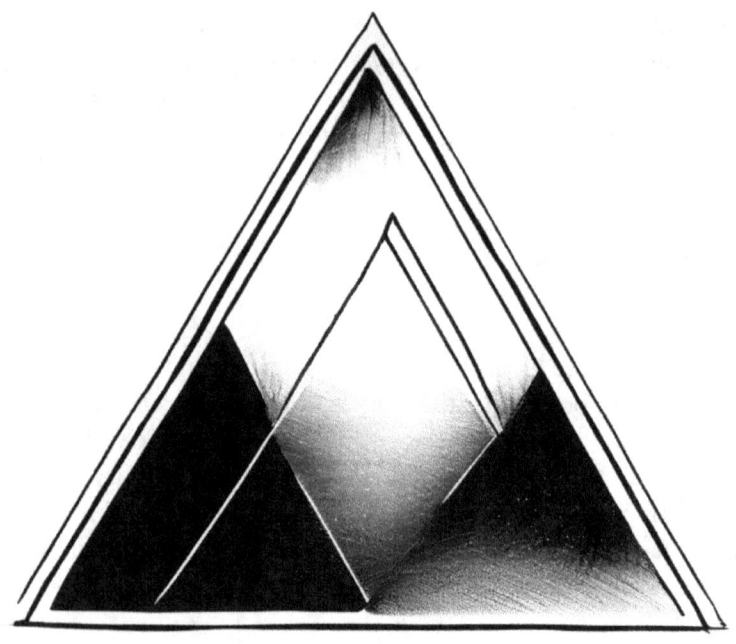

A simple tattoo design of a triangle

2. Change

While triangles are often associated with stability, they can also represent change and transformation. The triangle's sharp angles and dynamic structure suggest movement, making it a perfect symbol for transformation and evolution.
Many people opt for triangle tattoos to signify their personal journey through life's transitions, especially during periods of major change. For example, someone might choose a triangle tattoo after reaching an important milestone in their career or their now on the right direction. This design reminds them of their ability to adapt through life's natural corners.

A popular variation of this design is the upward-facing triangle, which can represent masculinity and the sun as it points toward the sky. Alternatively, a downward-facing triangle might symbolize femineity or reflection. Together, these variations convey the duality of change—both forward movement and introspection.

3. Spiritual Growth

Triangles are also closely tied to the idea of personal and spiritual growth. They can represent the journey toward self-discovery and pursuing higher goals or aspirations. The triangle's three points may symbolize different creative aspects of personal development, such as physical, emotional, and intellectual transformation.

For individuals wishing to depict their journey of self-discovery, a triangle tattoo can act as a perpetual symbol of their ongoing path. Triangles frequently weave into intricate tattoo designs, including mandalas and geometric motifs, underscoring their importance in the sphere of transformation and enlightenment. Such tattoos can serve not only as body art but also as great markers of one's evolving aspirations.

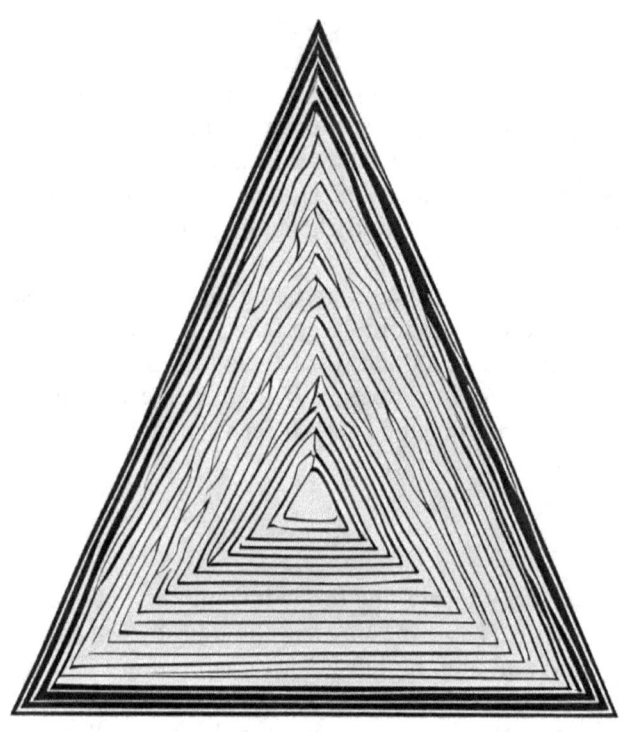

A tattoo design of an upward facing triangle

Circles: Eternity, Wholeness, Unity

1. Eternity

Circles are perhaps the most universally recognized shape. Due to their continuous, unbroken form, circles symbolize eternity. In contrast to shapes with sharp angles or defined endpoints, a circle has no beginning or end, making it a perfect representation of infinity or eternal cycles.
In tattoo art, circles often signify that life is cyclical, and endings are also beginnings. They can also represent unity and completion. People who get circle tattoos may do so to symbolize their understanding of life's continuous nature or to celebrate an unbreakable bond, whether with another person or with the universe itself.

2. Wholeness

Circles are frequently associated with the concepts of wholeness and completeness. Their perfectly balanced shape symbolizes totality and unity—whether it embodies the feeling of wholeness, the fulfillment of a goal, or the pursuit of perfection. A circle tattoo can signify self-acceptance or the notion of coming full circle in one's life journey. For individuals who have achieved a sense of balance or harmony, a circle often represents a feeling of completeness or inner peace.

A circle tattoo embodies completeness, reflecting the endless cycle of life. It also serves as a protective shield, guarding against negative influences while reinforcing an individual's sense of unity, strength, and positivity.

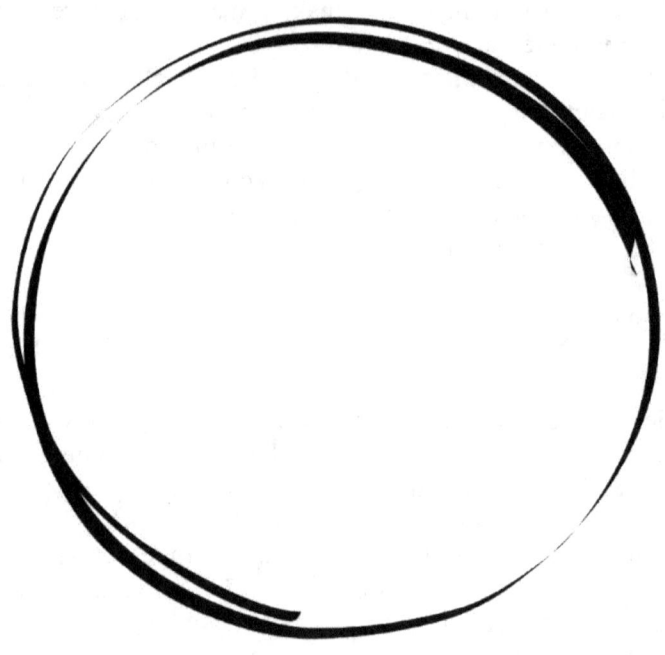

A simple tattoo idea of a circle

3. Unity

In tattoo designs, a circle often symbolizes the unity of different aspects of life, reflecting the deep connections between family members, friends, or a community. This emblematic shape emphasizes inclusivity, representing how individual experiences and diverse backgrounds come together to form a cohesive whole. The circle has no beginning or end, symbolizing eternal bonds and the cyclical nature of relationships. Whether it's a family gathering, communal gatherings, or friendships, this image serves as a reminder of shared experiences and mutual support. Each person represented within the circle adds to the richness of the collective narrative, highlighting the importance of connection, love, and belonging in our lives.

Mandalas: Spirituality, Balance, and Inner Peace

1. Spirituality

Mandalas are intricate designs built from concentric circles and symmetrical patterns. The word "mandala" means "circle," these designs embody a profound sense of completeness and balance. Many people are drawn to mandalas for their meditative qualities, often using them to reflect on life's interconnectedness. In tattooing, mandalas frequently represent a person's journey toward inner understanding and deeper self-awareness. Beyond their aesthetic appeal, many choose mandala tattoos for the deeper meanings they portray, symbolizing a quest for peace, balance, and personal growth. This spiritual aspect communicates with individuals on various levels, making mandalas a popular choice in body art.

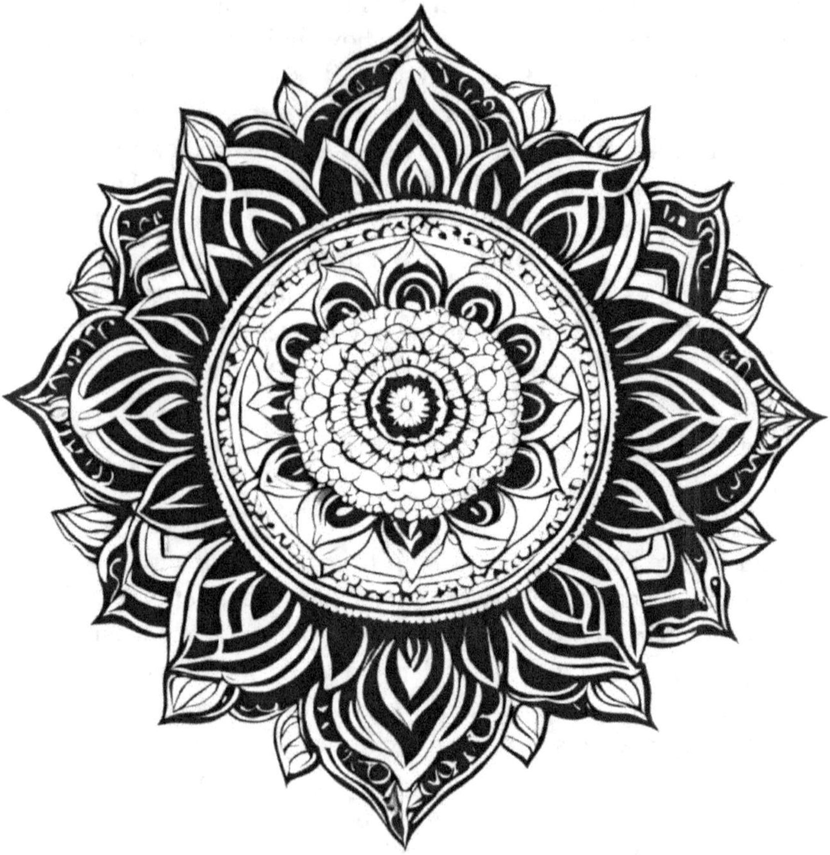

A tattoo design of a Mandala

2. Balance

Mandalas are often symmetrical, making them an ideal symbol of balance. Their intricate designs are arranged harmoniously, with every element carefully placed to maintain perfect symmetry. This balance reflects the individual's more profound desire for harmony in life, encompassing emotional, physical, and mental well-being. For people focused on achieving equilibrium in various aspects of their lives, a mandala tattoo can be a strong sign to maintain a balanced mindset. The design's symmetry creates a calming effect, promoting feelings of peace and centeredness. Some individuals choose mandalas to represent their journey toward balance, while others see the design as a metaphor for life's natural harmony and interconnectedness.

3. Inner Peace

The complexity of mandalas can also symbolize the search for inner peace. Their intricate patterns are often used in meditation and mindfulness practices, where focusing on the design can help bring about a sense of calm and focus. Mandalas carry the same strong associations with tranquility and deep reflection as tattoos. A mandala tattoo might remind the wearer to stay centered and grounded, even amid chaos and life's unpredictability. It can symbolize the wearer's commitment to self-reflection and the ongoing pursuit of inner peace. For many, the mandala represents a visual element and a lifelong discovery toward understanding oneself more profoundly and achieving a sense of peace and serenity in everyday life.

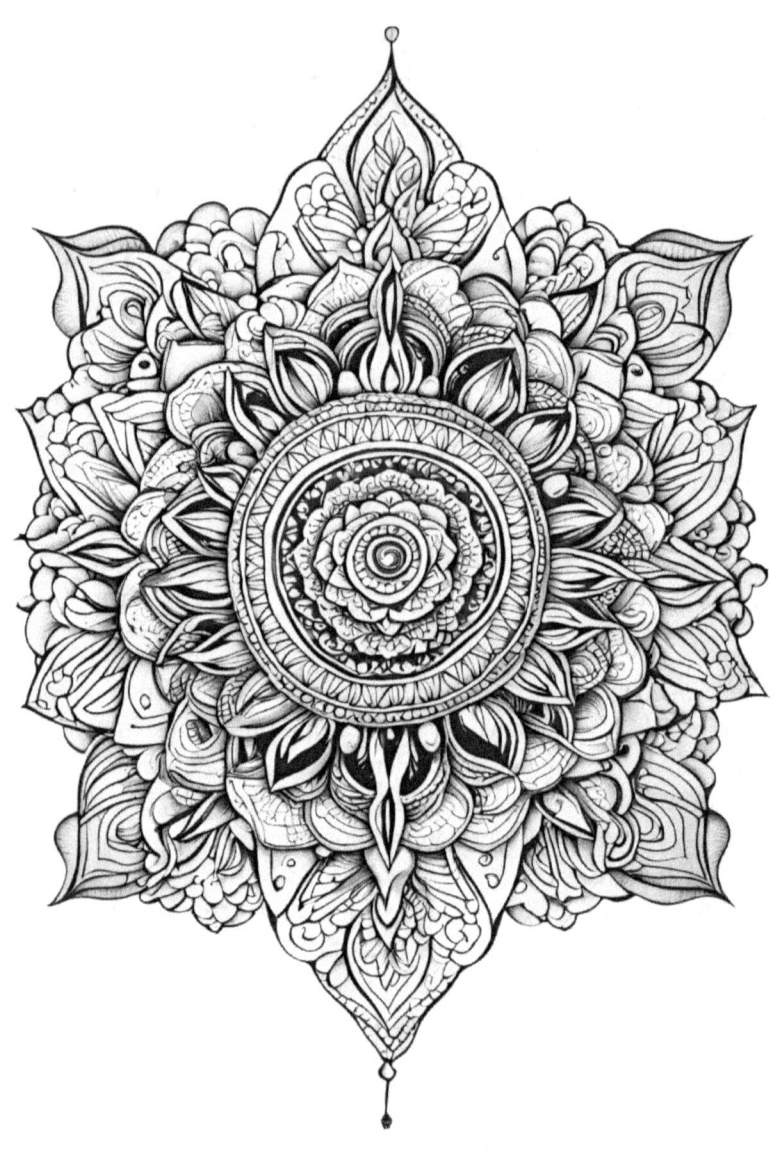

An alternate tattoo design of a mandala

Abstract Symbols: Freedom, Uniqueness, and Individuality

1. Freedom

Abstract symbols are the perfect canvas for expressing freedom, inviting open interpretation, and disregarding strict rules. This flexibility allows for a vast array of creativity, making the meaning behind abstract tattoos as fluid as the designs themselves. Many abstract tattoos incorporate lines, shapes, and forms that symbolize liberation—be it from societal expectations, struggles, or other constraints that feel confining. For instance, abstract line work may embody the freedom to explore new ideas, embrace risks, or break away from tradition. Swirls and waves can symbolize movement and fluidity, illustrating that life is not linear but ever-changing. Individuals who opt for abstract symbols often seek to express their unique freedom and individuality without being restricted by rigid meanings.

2. Uniqueness

One of the most compelling reasons for choosing an abstract tattoo is the opportunity to create something entirely unique. Abstract designs defy conventional forms, allowing the wearer to tailor the artwork to their tastes and experiences. Because abstract tattoos are open to interpretation, they provide an avenue for the wearer to communicate their identity in a deeply personal and meaningful way. These tattoos visually represent the wearer's individuality through intricate shapes, bold lines, or unconventional patterns. They can symbolize creativity, self-expression, and a distinctive perspective on life that sets them apart from others.

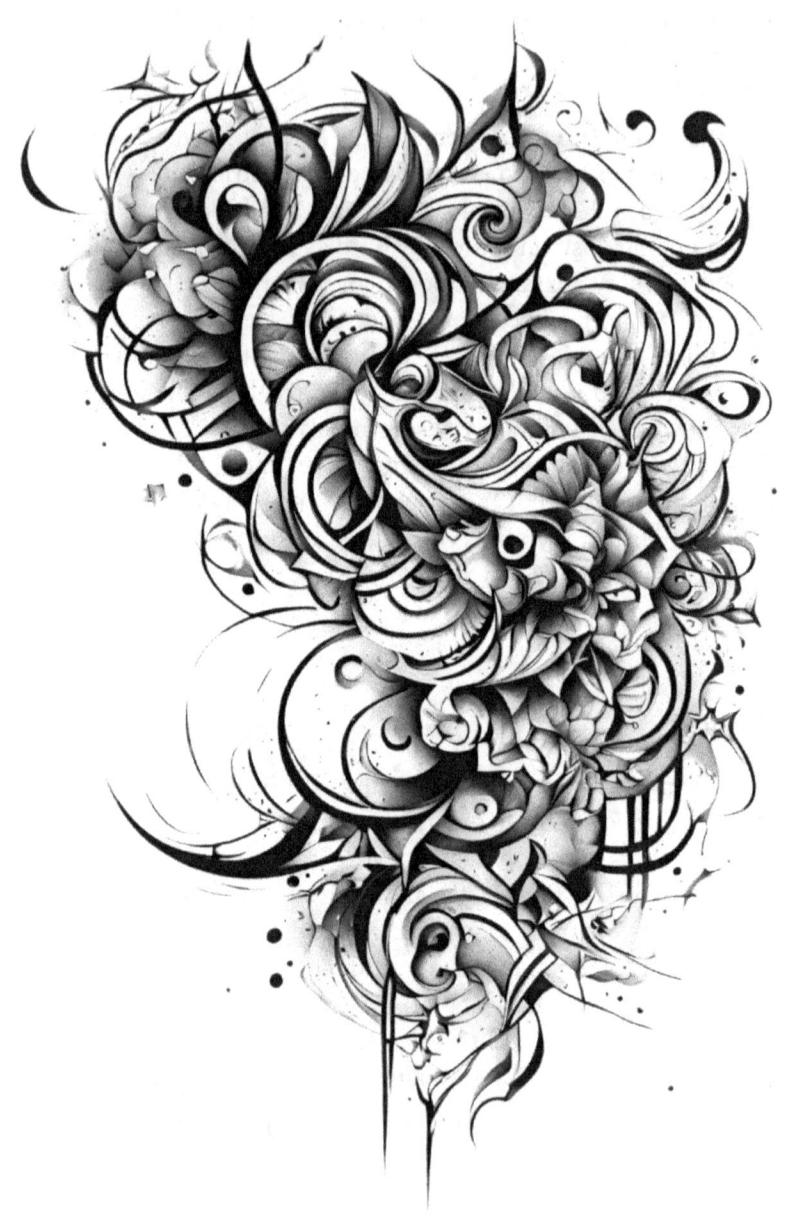

An example of an abstract tattoo design

3. Individuality

Abstract symbols are a natural choice for people who want tattoos to reflect their unique identity. These tattoos are often designed without a specific reference point, making them different and one-of-a-kind. Some abstract tattoos utilize shapes, lines, or patterns that are distinctive to the individual. In contrast, others draw inspiration from art, nature, or even emotional experiences, creating subjective tattoo bodyart

For some, an abstract tattoo may represent their self-discovery, encapsulating pivotal moments or feelings. In contrast, for others, it might reflect their outlook on life and the world around them. The abstract nature of these tattoos allows for endless creativity, ensuring that no two designs are exactly alike. By choosing an abstract tattoo, individuals can proudly embrace their uniqueness and showcase their individuality through this deeply personal form of body art.

Chapter Conclusion

In conclusion, geometric and abstract tattoos serve as a compelling medium for expressing individuality and deeper narratives. Through the precise lines of triangles, the endless elegance of circles, the intricate designs of mandalas, and the fluidity of abstract forms, these tattoos allow individuals to articulate their beliefs and feelings. Each geometric shape carries its own connotation, and even subtle alterations in design can unveil fresh interpretations, amplifying their importance. For anyone in search of a timeless art form that speaks volumes, these tattoos transcend mere decoration, becoming vivid stories inscribed on the body that reflect the wearer's unique identity.

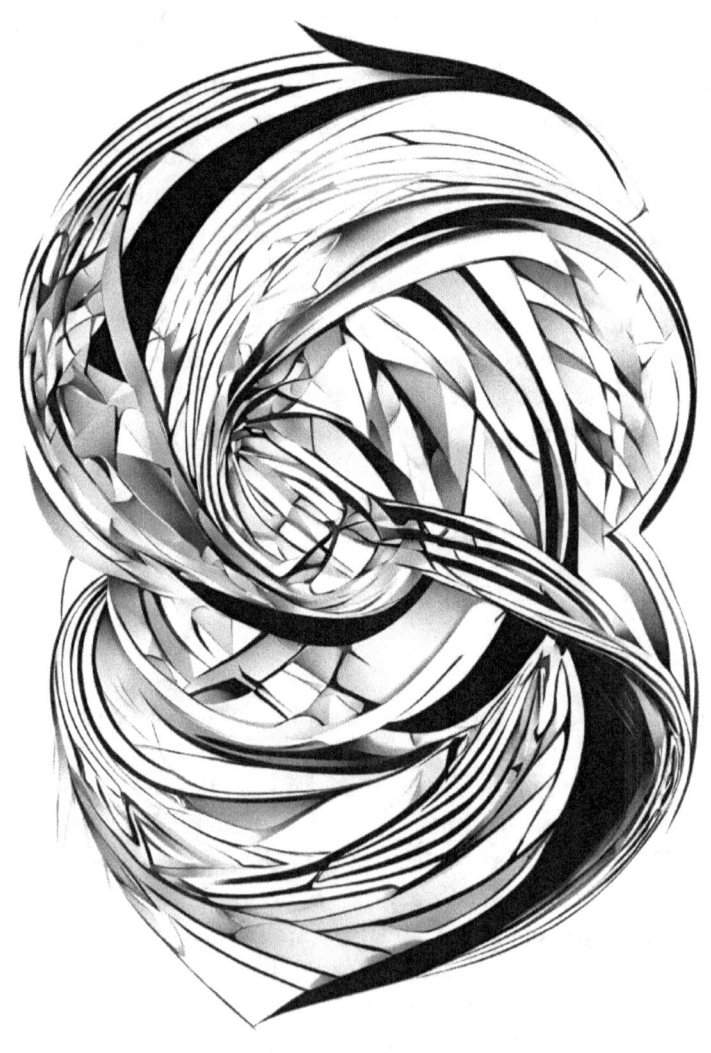

An example of an abstract tattoo design

Chapter 3: Celestial and Elemental Tattoos

Celestial and elemental tattoos are inspired by nature and the universe, offering a unique blend of art and meaning. They symbolize our deepest desires, emotions, and connections to the universe around us. These tattoos transcend cultural boundaries, allowing individuals to express universally understood meanings. From the sun and moon to the elements of fire and water, celestial and elemental tattoos carry rich symbolism and signal a strong connection to the natural and cosmic forces that govern life. In this chapter, we will explore the meanings of various celestial and elemental symbols, delving into the stories they convey through tattoos.

Sun: Power, Vitality, Enlightenment

1. Power

The sun is a universal symbol of power, energy, and life. Its constant presence in the sky provides warmth, light, and sustenance, making it a central force of existence throughout the ages. In many cultures, the sun is seen for its ability to create and sustain life, symbolizing strength, authority, and inspiration across various myths and legends. As a tattoo, the sun often represents personal power, vitality, and light, reminding one to embrace inner power. The sun stands as an emblem of individual endurance and vitality, representing a source of never-ending heat, energy and positivity. It invites reflection on one's aspirations and serves as a guide, illuminating the path to success and fulfillment. Furthermore, the sun's cycles mirror the rhythms of life, emphasizing growth, rebirth, and change, which are integral to the path of empowerment.

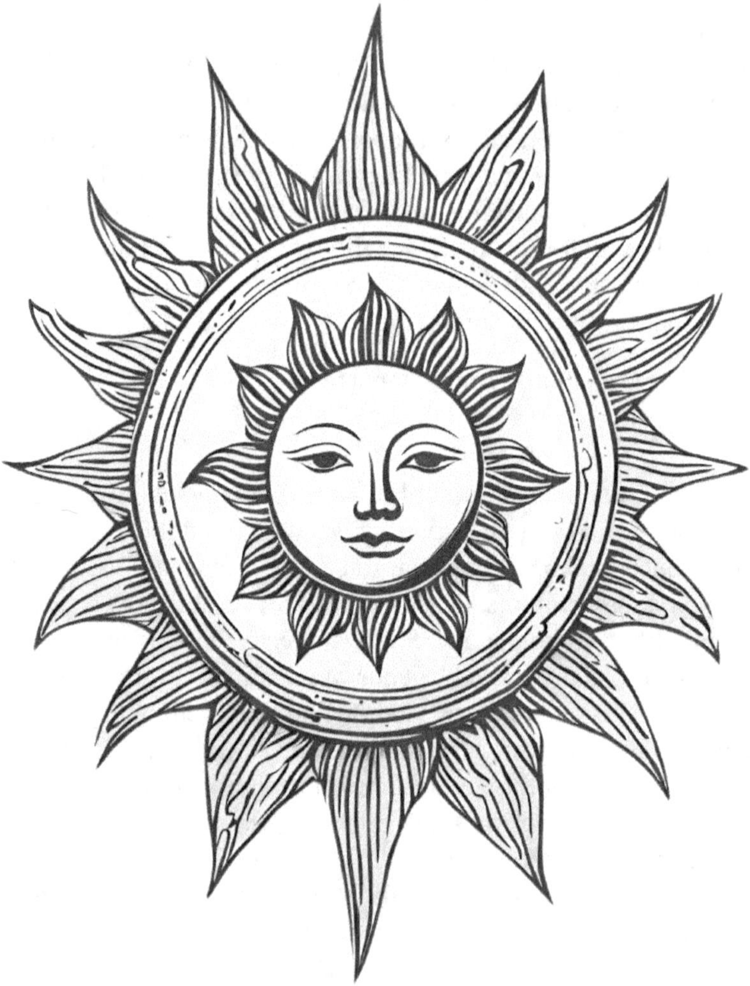

A tattoo design of a sun

2. Vitality

The sun's life-giving energy symbolizes vitality and rejuvenation, embodying the profound essence of renewal. Each new day unfolds with fresh opportunities and experiences, illuminating the potential to restart and improve. For those who see themselves as resilient, the sun tattoo designs can implicate the capacity to rise above adversity, radiating warmth and life like its celestial counterpart. A sun tattoo can signify a new beginning or a revived sense of purpose, becoming a powerful sign of boundless energy and perseverance. Many also connect sun tattoos to adventure and exploration, embodying the spirit of discovering new horizons.

3. Enlightenment

The sun's light is intrinsically linked to knowledge and enlightenment, driving away darkness and revealing hidden truths, thus serving as a beacon of hope and clarity. It symbolizes wisdom, revelation, and illumination in both a literal and metaphorical sense. Those on a quest for regeneration may choose a sun tattoo to signify their journey toward enlightenment, acknowledging the trials and triumphs that shape their understanding. In this context, the sun reminds us to pursue the light, embrace wisdom, and seek clarity in life, encouraging us to illuminate our minds and hearts. Whether exploring self-discovery or striving for intellectual heights, the sun powerfully represents your commitment to truth and light, guiding you toward self-realization. It rekindles a sense of wonder about the world around us, urging us to remain curious and open-minded, ultimately enriching our lives with more profound meaning and insight.

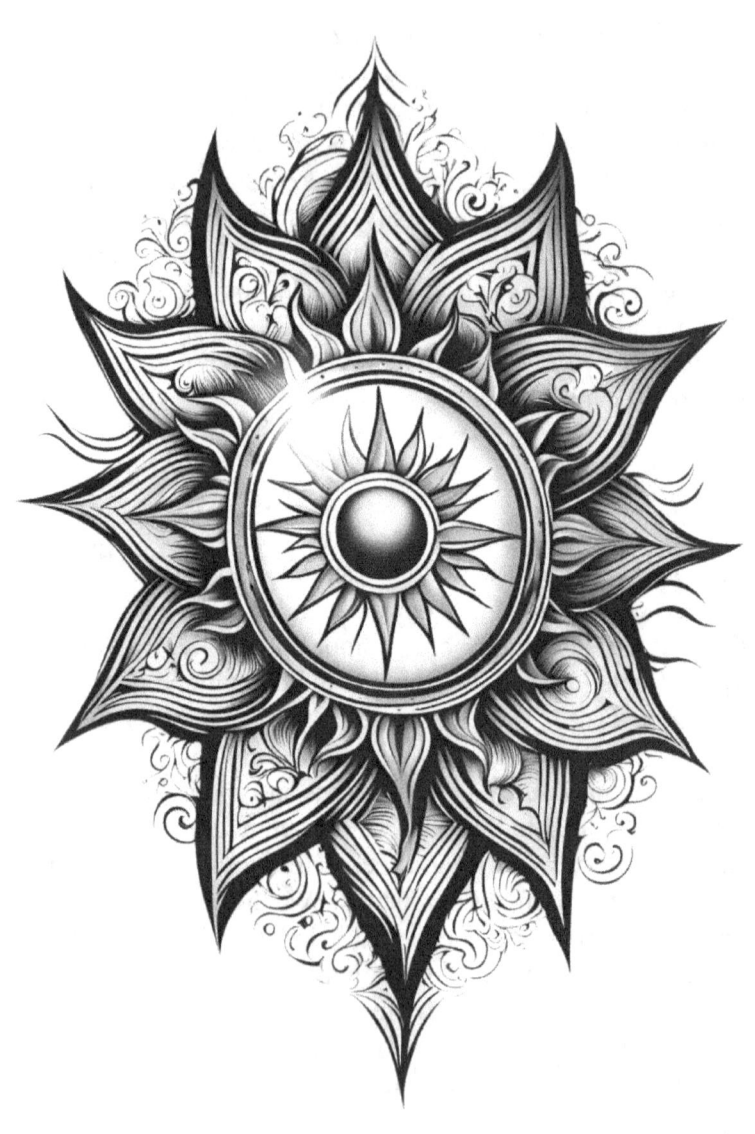

A tattoo design of a sun

Moon: Intuition, Femininity, Change

1. Intuition

The moon has forever been a beacon of intuition and the deeper layers of the subconscious. Its shifting phases ripple through the tides and the rhythms of our world, believed to influence our emotions and inner reflections significantly. A moon tattoo often symbolizes a profound bond with one's true self and the intuitive forces guiding us. Moon tattoos are about ones emotional connection and harmony with the nature environment. The moon embodies the art of tuning into one's instincts, navigating life's intricate paths, and trusting the inner voice that leads us through light and shadow. This connection fosters personal reflection and sparks emotional transformation, enriching our comprehension of ourselves and the universe around us.

2. Femininity

Historically, the moon has been a powerful emblem of femininity. Many cultures celebrate the moon as a nurturing and emotionally rich symbol. Individuals seeking to honor their feminine essence or showcase qualities like empathy, sensitivity, and emotional strength often choose moon tattoos. These designs are striking representations of life's cyclical nature, emphasizing our ability to endure, evolve, and thrive through the ever-changing phases of existence. Furthermore, they highlight the importance of celebrating one's individuality.

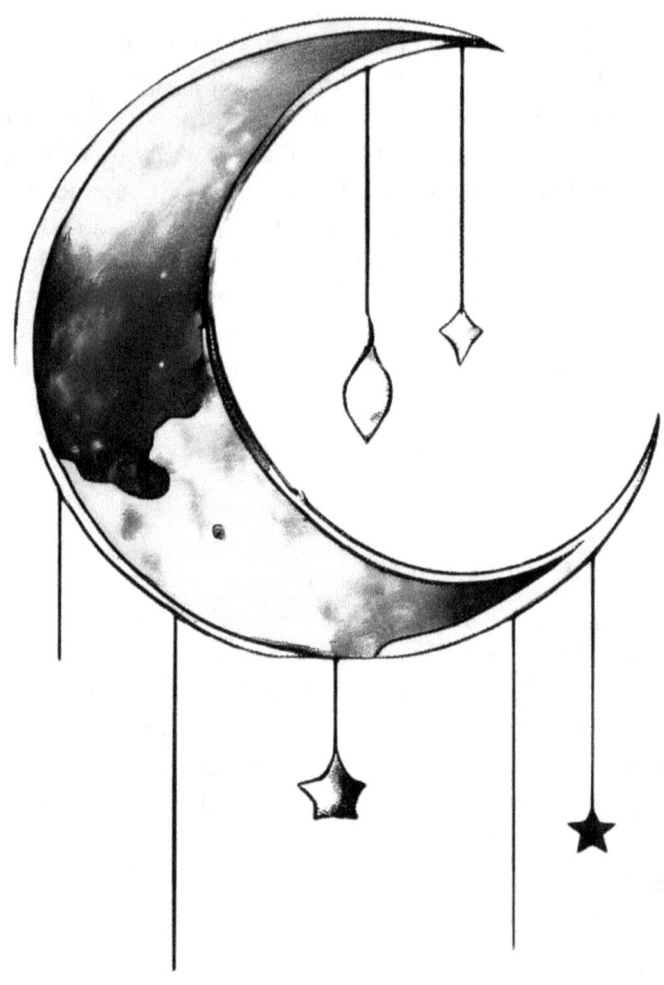

A tattoo design of a moon

3. Change

The moon's waxing and waning phases make it a powerful symbol of change and transformation. Its constant movement through the night sky reflects the profound idea that nothing stays the same forever. People experiencing personal growth, transformation, or significant life transitions might choose a moon tattoo to signify their ability to adapt and evolve gracefully. The moon serves as a reminder that life is fluid and ever-changing. Just as the moon transitions through its various phases, individuals navigate different life stages, each with their own phases and lessons. A moon tattoo can beautifully represent the belief that personal transformation is a natural and continuous process.

Stars and Constellations: Guidance, Ambition, Dreams

1. Guidance

Stars have been used for centuries as navigational tools, guiding sailors and travelers through the vast night sky. As tattoos, stars can symbolize guidance, protection, and the idea of finding one's way, literally and metaphorically. A star tattoo can represent the powerful notion of following a guiding light through difficult times or staying on the right path in life. People who choose this design may do so because they see themselves as being guided by something larger than themselves—whether that's their intuition, their goals, or the supportive people in their lives. These celestial symbols can inspire ambition and dreams, reminding wearers of their potential to illuminate their adventures in the right direction.

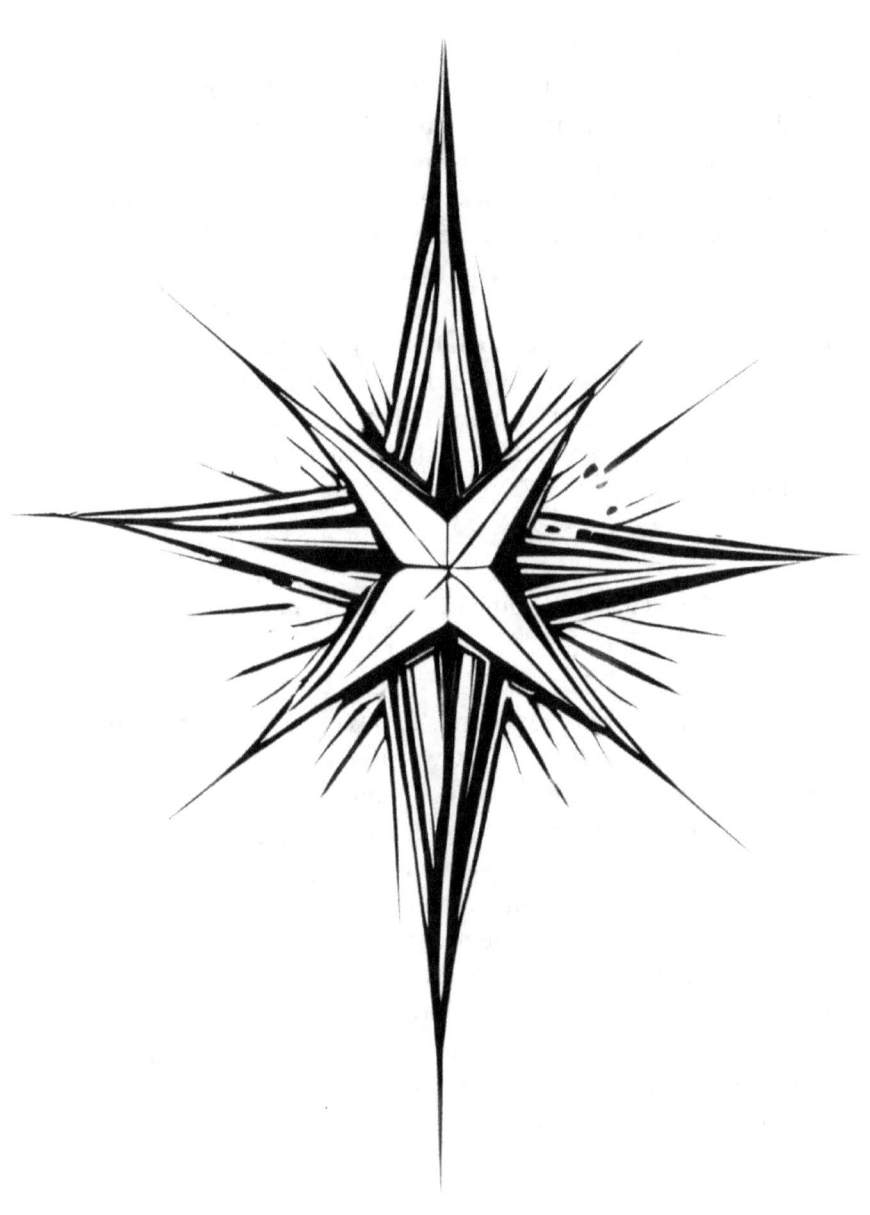

A star tattoo design

2. Ambition

Stars are often synonymous with ambition and the relentless pursuit of one's dreams. The expressive phrase "reaching for the stars" encapsulates this idea beautifully, inspiring individuals to aim for their highest aspirations. Each star in the night sky represents not just a distant fire but the possibility of realizing one's fullest potential. Star tattoos often resonate with those who are passionate about their goals. Whether etched as a solitary star or crafted into a breathtaking constellation, these designs are daily reminders of one's ambition and the unwavering focus needed to chase dreams. Each point of light can symbolize a unique aspiration, illuminating the path toward achieving personal greatness.

3. Dreams

Beyond mere ambition, stars embody the essence of dreams and the boundless realm of imagination. In various cultures, they act as a bridge between the tangible and the ethereal, representing hope, inspiration, and the pursuit of the extraordinary. A star tattoo can signify a person's innermost desires, becoming a visual promise to never stop dreaming. It encourages individuals to hold tightly to life's inherent magic and mystery. Constellation tattoos, in particular, conjure a sense of wonder, beautifully illustrating how we are interconnected with the universe. Each star within a constellation might symbolize a different life goal or different successes one has achieved or is striving for. Stars are a popular choice among tattoo body art when representing ones dreams and ambitions.

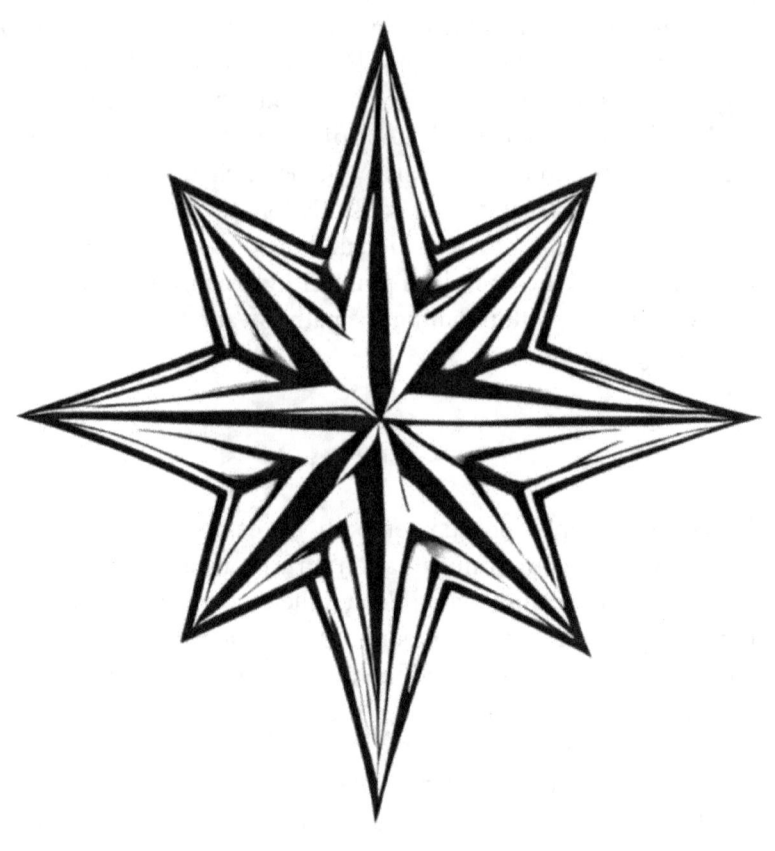

A star tattoo design

Planets: Exploration, Discovery, Beauty

1. Exploration

Planets embody the essence of exploration and discovery, symbolizing both the adventurous spirit of space travel and the profound personal journey of uncovering new aspects of oneself. A tattoo of a planet may beautifully capture an individual's curiosity and desire to wander into the unknown, whether in the physical realm of the universe or the intricate landscape of their psyche. Those who choose planet tattoos often possess a bold sense of adventure and an insatiable thirst for knowledge, reflecting their unwavering passion for exploration—both of the surrounding environment and their inner selves.

2. Discovery

As potent symbols, planets invite the discovery of unprecedented possibilities and transformative ideas. In tattoo art, they highlight a profound willingness to embrace new perspectives, beliefs, and exhilarating experiences. Each planet represents a piece of the vast tapestry of life, encouraging wearers to remain open-minded and receptive to unexpected insights.

3. Beauty

Planet tattoos beautifully capture the vastness and mystery of the cosmos. Each design reflects the unique characteristics of celestial bodies, reminding us of the elegance of the universe. These tattoos symbolize our connection to the stars, offering a personal narrative of exploration and wonder, showcasing the infinite beauty that surrounds us.

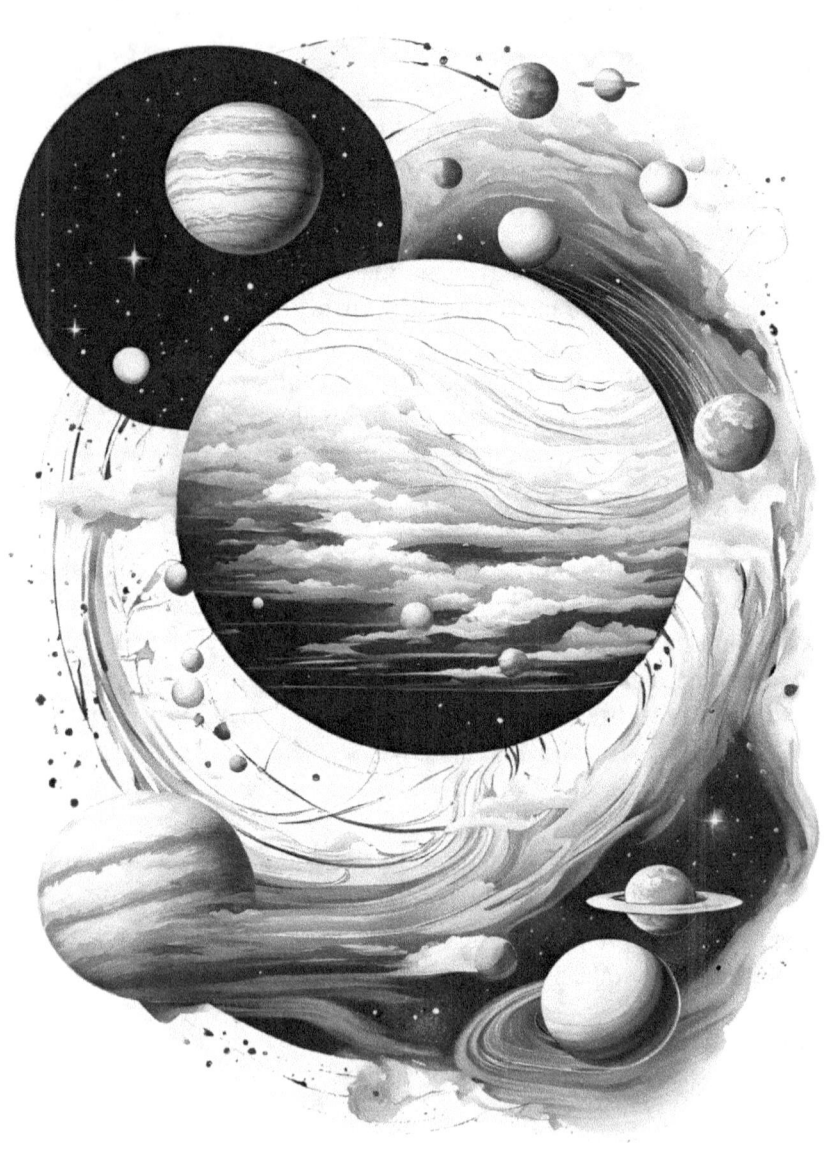

A planetary tattoo design

Fire: Transformation, Passion, Energy

1. Transformation

Fire tattoos symbolize transformation and renewal, embodying the powerful cycle of destruction and rebirth. Just as fire can consume and obliterate, it also sparks change and growth, reminding us that even in life's toughest moments, there is potential for new beginnings. The vibrant flames in these designs evoke passion, strength and anger. Fire tattoos serve as a personal emblem of personal evolution, encouraging individuals to embrace their journeys and transformations. Ultimately, they reflect the dynamic nature of life itself, where change is not only inevitable but beautiful.

2. Passion

Fire's intense, burning energy makes it a potent symbol of passion and desire. Whether directed towards love, career, hobbies, or personal goals, fire tattoos often reflect a deep commitment to what truly matters. For those who embrace life with vigor and enthusiasm, a fire tattoo captures that spirit, symbolizing their fiery nature and the ability to channel passions into transformative endeavors. It can also represent the flames of inspiration that fuel creativity and drive.

3. Energy

Fire embodies raw, uncontainable energy—dynamic, ever-moving, and never static. A fire tattoo can signify a person's vibrant energy, relentless drive, and determination to keep advancing despite obstacles. Fire is the perfect symbol for individuals eager to express their boundless enthusiasm and unyielding motivation. It indicates their inner fire—an unstoppable force propelling them to achieve their goals, live with intensity, and embrace life with passion and energy.

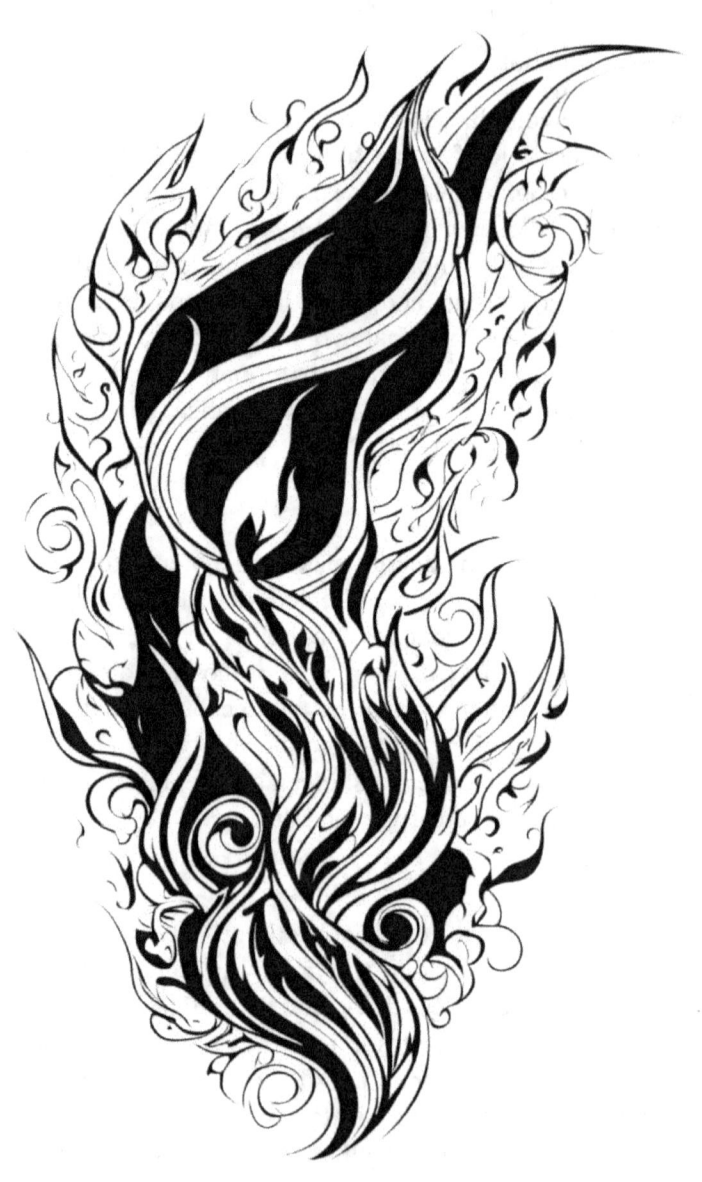

A conceptual fire tattoo design

Water: Renewal, Emotional Depth, Adaptability

1. Renewal

Water is a profound emblem of renewal and cleansing, embodying the constant flow of life. Its malleable nature symbolizes the release of the old to welcome the new. A tattoo depicting water—be it a gentle wave or an intricate waterfall. It reflects the innate desire to embrace change, cleanse away past burdens, and move forward with clarity and purpose. Like a river that carves new paths through the landscape, this tattoo captures the essence of continuous movement and evolution.

2. Emotional Depth

Water intricately connects to emotions and the subconscious, mirroring the complexities of human experience. Its fluid, shifting characteristics symbolize the vast depths of feelings we can encounter. For those who wish to express their emotional journeys, a water tattoo can capture this—it speaks to the flow of emotions and sensitivity. It beautifully encapsulates the struggle and serenity in navigating life's emotional tides, making it a meaningful representation of one's inner self.

3. Adaptability

Water's remarkable ability to conform to any shape or path signifies adaptability and freedom. A water-inspired tattoo embodies the strength to flow through life, adapting to various circumstances with grace and flexibility. This symbol constantly reminds one of one's fluidity, encouraging individuals to embrace change and thrive amid uncertainty. Choosing water as a tattoo signifies a commitment to navigate life's storms while maintaining peace and purpose, encouraging an adaptable way of life.

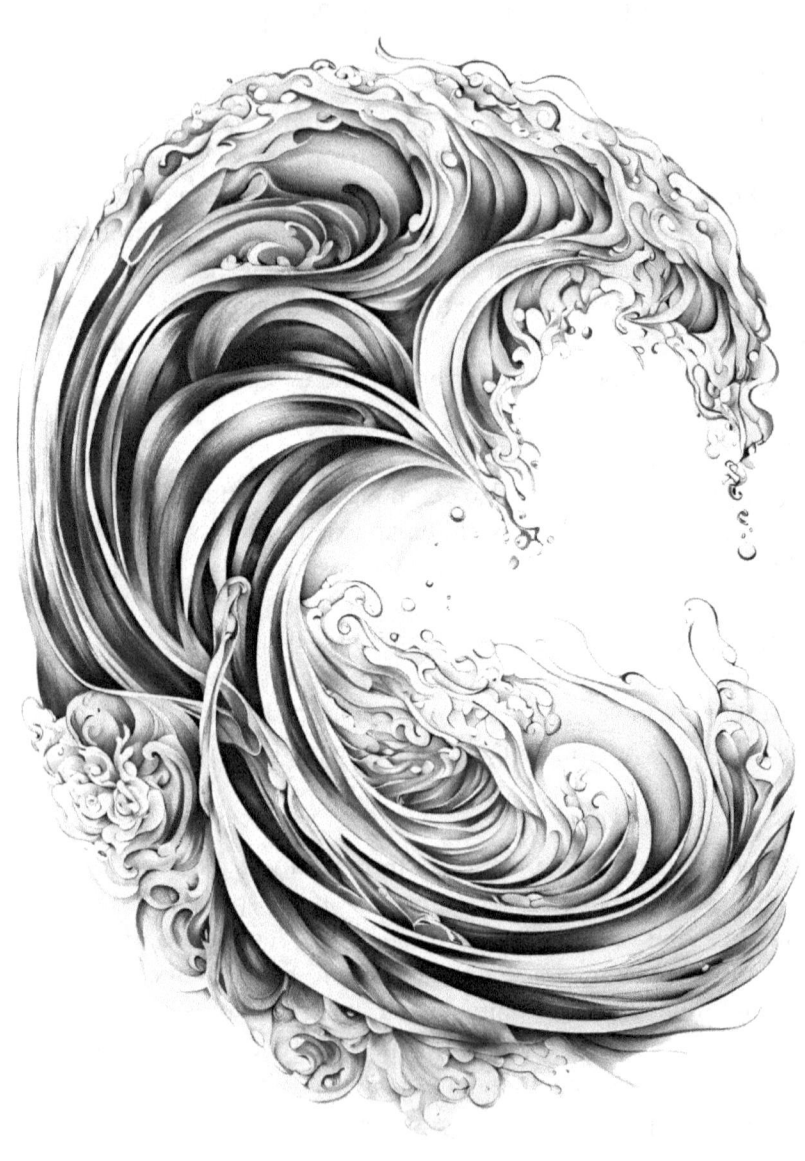

A tattoo design of water

Air: Freedom, Communication, Intelligence

1. Freedom

Air is often associated with freedom and the ability to move without constraints. It represents the idea of breaking free from limitations and exploring new physical and mental possibilities. An air tattoo can symbolize someone's desire for freedom, independence, and the ability to live life on their own terms.

Whether it's a simple gust of wind or a more intricate depiction of clouds or birds, air tattoos reflect a person's need to feel unbound and free. They are indicators of the importance of living a life that isn't confined by others' expectations or restrictions.

2. Communication

Air is also connected to communication; it carries sound and enables us to share ideas and information. An air tattoo might represent someone's belief in the power of words, thoughts, and expression.

For those who value clear communication and the ability to connect with others through language, an air tattoo can symbolize their communicative skills. It can also reflect a commitment to honesty, openness, and transparency in relationships and interactions.

3. Intelligence

Air's association with the mind and intellect makes it a symbol of intelligence and intellectual pursuits. People who choose air tattoos may do so to represent their curiosity, their love of learning, and their intelligence.

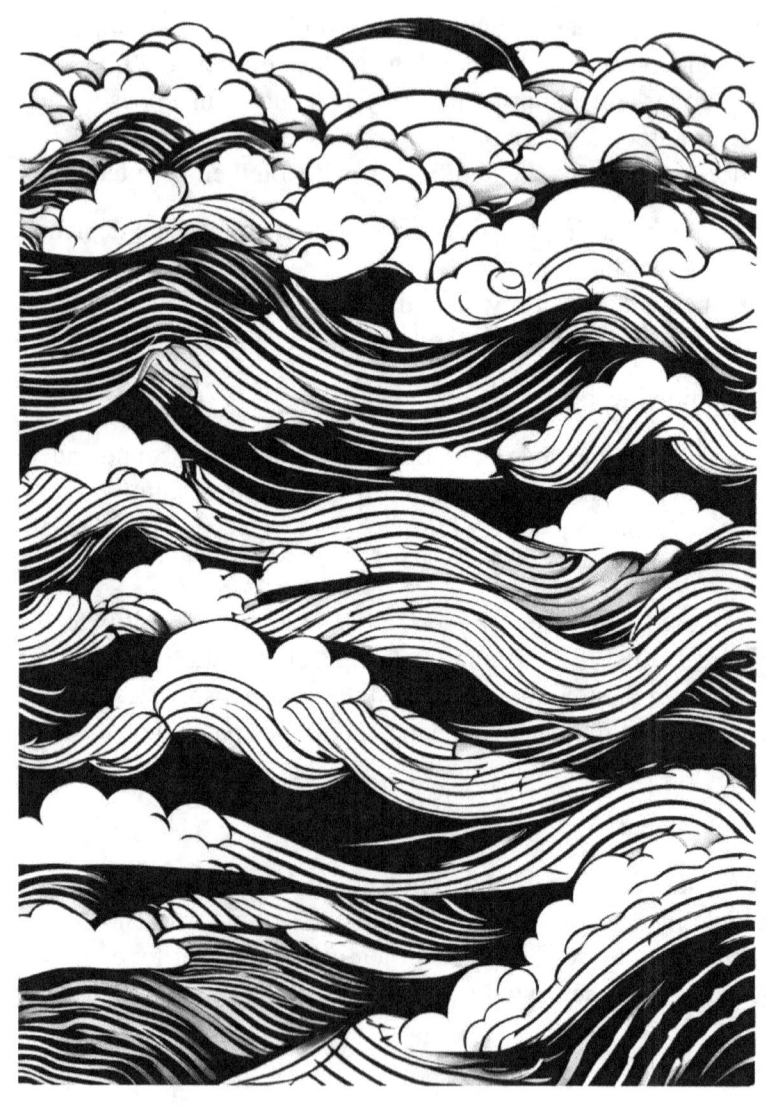

A tattoo concept of air

Lightning: Sudden Change, Power, Inspiration

1. Sudden Change

Lightning embodies the idea of swift, unexpected transformation. Its bright, transient nature symbolizes how life can change in the blink of an eye, introducing new viewpoints and experiences. A lightning tattoo can represent an individual's decisiveness and their capacity to adapt swiftly to everyday situations.

2. Power

The immense, awe-inspiring force of lightning symbolizes intense speed, unparalleled strength, and raw power. A lightning tattoo can represent a person's determination and strong resolve to harness their full potential quickly and at an impressive pace. For those who see themselves as formidable or persistently driven, this tattoo serves as a powerful emblem of strength, conveying a profound message of empowerment and purposeful progression. It serves as a source of motivation to push boundaries and embrace one's inner energy.

3. Creativity

Often viewed as a spark of sudden creativity or insight, lightning represents those enlightening moments we often refer to as "lightning bolt" revelations. A lightning tattoo may symbolize someone's artistic flair, quick thinking, or moments of brilliance that drive new ideas and projects forward. For individuals who embrace their imaginative side or find inspiration in bursts of energy, this tattoo becomes a vivid reminder of the powerful sparks that fuel their passions and pursuits. With each flash, it celebrates the beauty of creativity and the potential it holds.

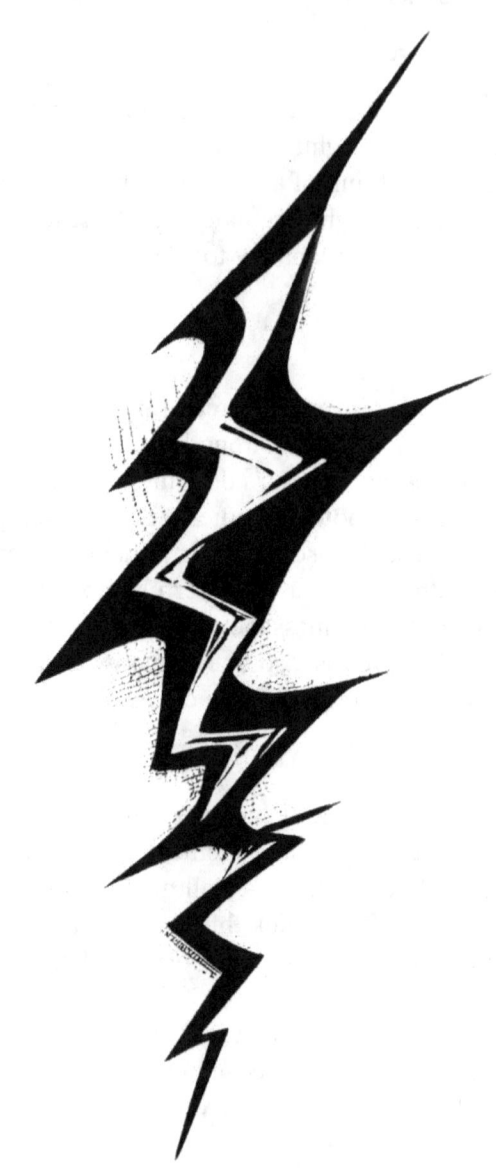

A lightning bolt tattoo design

Comets: Rare Moments, Important Events

1. Rare Moments

Comets, with their brief yet breathtaking appearances in the night sky, symbolize those extraordinary instances that ignite our imagination. They encapsulate fleeting experiences that can forever change our perspective on life. Each comet carries with it a captivating story — a journey of wonder. A comet tattoo can be a meaningful emblem of those rare events or pivotal experiences that have indelibly shaped one's identity. By commemorating these unique moments, individuals passionately celebrate the beauty of change and the transient nature of life, reminding themselves that even the briefest encounters can leave a profound and lasting impact.

2. Important Events

Beyond representing rare moments, comets are profound symbols of vital life events that deserve heartfelt recognition. A comet tattoo can beautifully mark a significant chapter in one's life. It embodies the joy, unknown, and transformation that come with pivotal moments in our journey. It is a fantastic tattoo idea for the individual interested in astronomy and space. Comet tattoos often represent hope, renewal, and the fleeting nature of time. They remind us to embrace change and celebrate moments of brilliance in our lives, highlighting exploration. Each comet in ink invites reflection and gratitude for the chapters defining who we are.

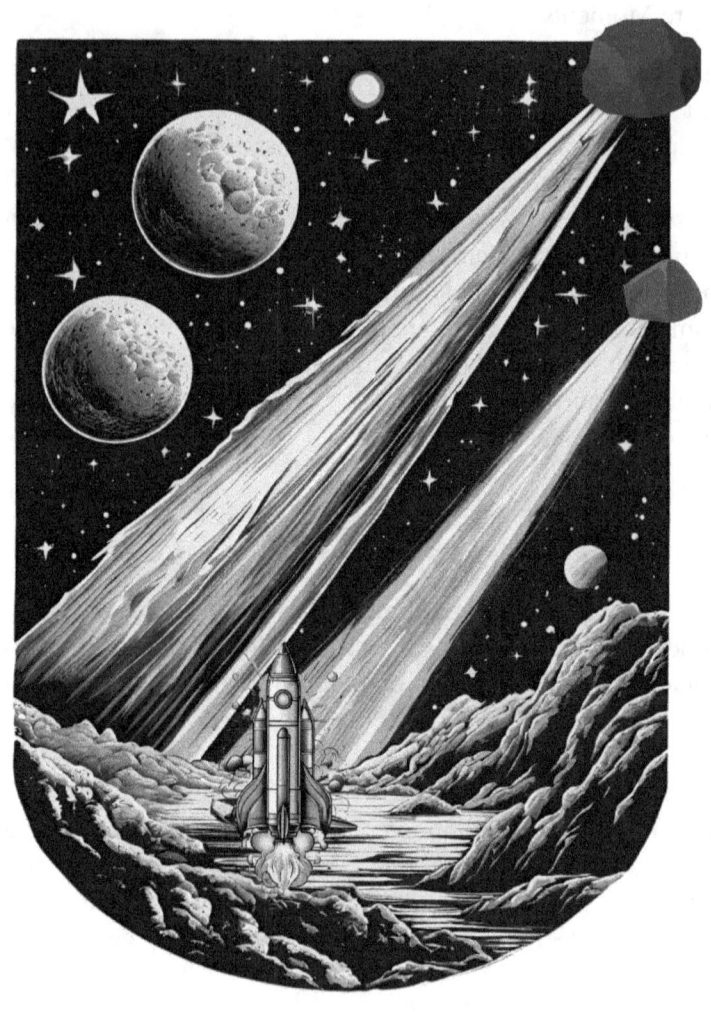

A comet and space conceptual tattoo design

Galaxies: Infinity, Exploration, The Unknown

1. Infinity

Galaxies, with their vast, endless expanse, are symbols of infinity and the boundless nature of the universe. A galaxy tattoo can represent someone's belief in limitless possibilities and the idea that there are no boundaries to what they can achieve. For individuals who wish to get an infinity tattoo they exhibit endless potential and a galaxy tattoo expresses their limitless nature. It reflects the belief that new opportunities and adventures are always waiting to be discovered. Moreover, galaxy designs' swirling colors and intricate patterns can promote feelings of wonder and awe, inspiring individuals to pursue their dreams fearlessly. Each star within a galaxy may symbolize specific aspirations or cherished memories.

2. Exploration

Galaxies also symbolize exploration in the vast physical realm of space. A galaxy tattoo can represent a person's innate desire to explore the unknown through travel or learning. For those driven by curiosity and a love for adventure, a galaxy tattoo embodies their adventurous spirit, capturing the essence of the endless journey of exploration. This emblematic ink constantly motivates the wearer to venture beyond their comfort zones, encouraging them to seek new experiences and invaluable knowledge. It beautifully encapsulates the thrill of uncovering hidden facets of life and oneself and reminds us that we are only an infinitesimal part of the vast universe. Ultimately, these elements combine to make a galaxy tattoo a powerful statement of individuality, aspiration, and the boundless possibilities that await.

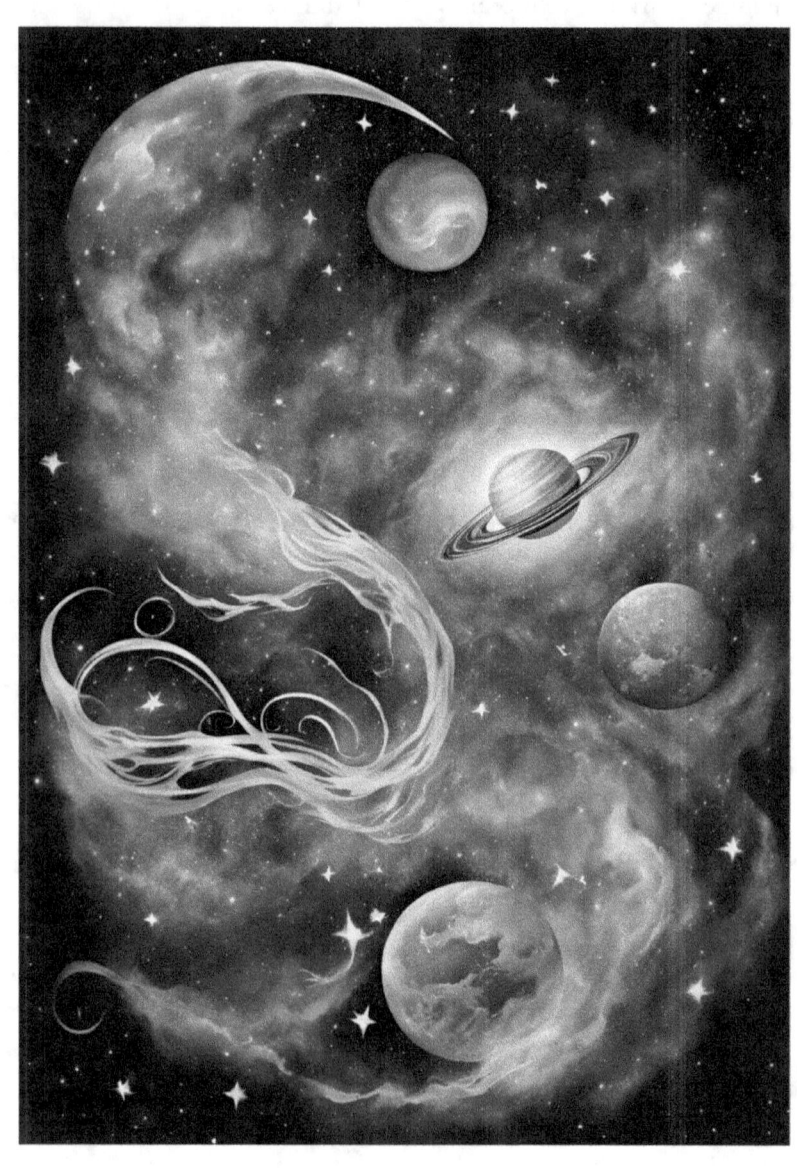

A mythical galaxy tattoo design

3. The Unknown

The mystery of galaxies often symbolizes the unknown and uncharted territories of life. A galaxy tattoo can represent a person's comfort with uncertainty, willingness to embrace the unpredictable, and belief in the inherent beauty of life's mysteries. For those who find inspiration in the unknown, a galaxy tattoo is an interesting sign that not everything in life can or should be fully understood. It celebrates the wonder, curiosity, and excitement accompanying the unknown, encouraging individuals to explore new possibilities and face challenges with an open heart and mind. Ultimately, it embodies life's discovery, inviting adventure and introspection.

Chapter Conclusion

Celestial and elemental tattoos offer a rich variety of symbolism, drawing from the natural and cosmic forces that shape our existence. Each design, whether it's the radiant sun, the ever-changing moon, or the fiery force of lightning, carries unique meanings with universal truths. Whether you seek to express vitality, intuition, ambition, or adaptability, celestial and elemental tattoos provide timeless symbols to reflect who you are and the adventure you're on.

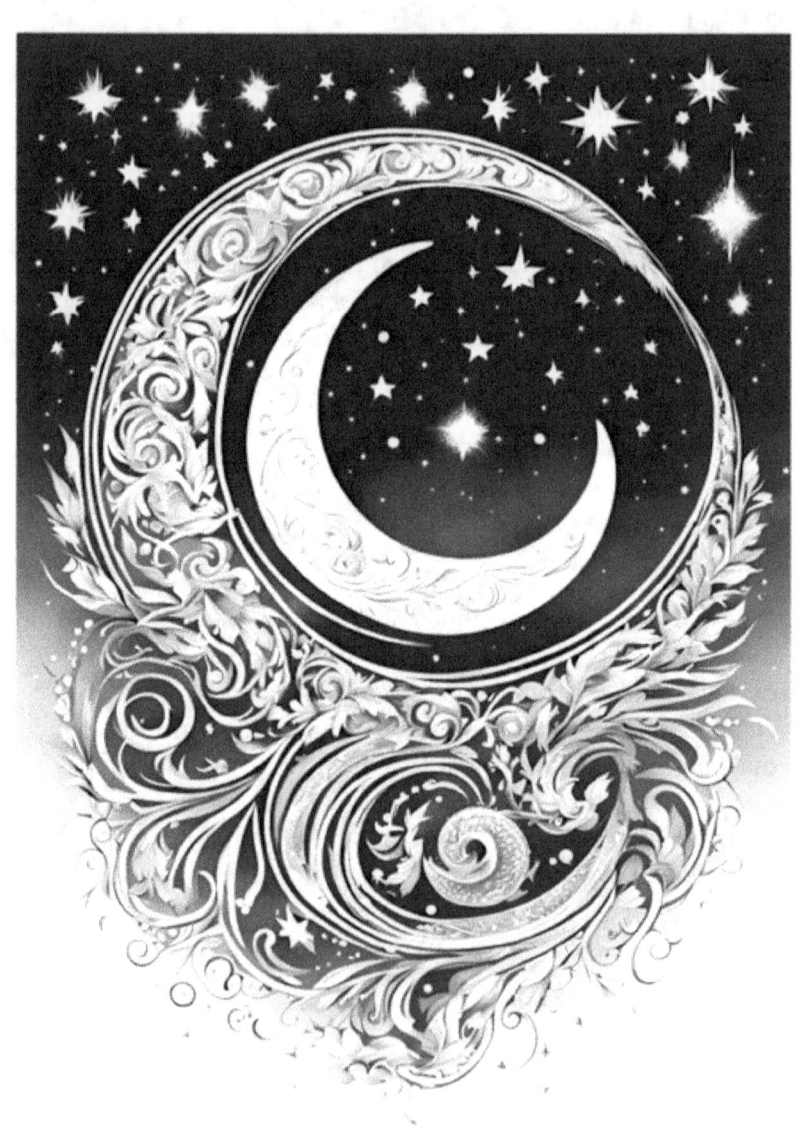

A celestial tattoo concept

Chapter 4: Mythical Creatures and Fantasy Tattoos

Mythical creatures have long captured the human imagination, representing a blend of reality and fantasy that speaks to our core emotions, desires, and fears. Fantasy tattoos featuring mythical creatures like dragons, phoenixes, unicorns, and more carry symbolic meanings that often reflect traits like power, adaptability, purity, and freedom. These creatures, which span the mythologies and folklore of cultures across the world, provide imagery for those who want to embody larger-than-life qualities.

In this chapter, we will explore the various mythical creatures and their associated meanings, providing insight into the stories behind them and how they resonate with people today.

Dragons: Power, Protection, Wisdom

1. Power

Dragons are one of the most iconic mythical creatures, symbolizing immense power, energy and dominance. In many cultures, particularly in East Asia, dragons are revered as symbols of natural forces, such as the sky, sea, or storms. In Western traditions, dragons often appear as fearsome creatures guarding treasures, further emphasizing their association with raw power and control.

Individuals opting for dragon tattoos often find that the symbolism embodies immense physical might and personal empowerment. A dragon design can represent one's toughness and unwavering resolve. Frequently depicted as fierce and unbridled, the dragon tattoo captures that spirit, illustrating a sense of autonomy and fearless determination. It represents a connection to ferocity and mythical wisdom, inspiring those who wear it to embrace their true potential.

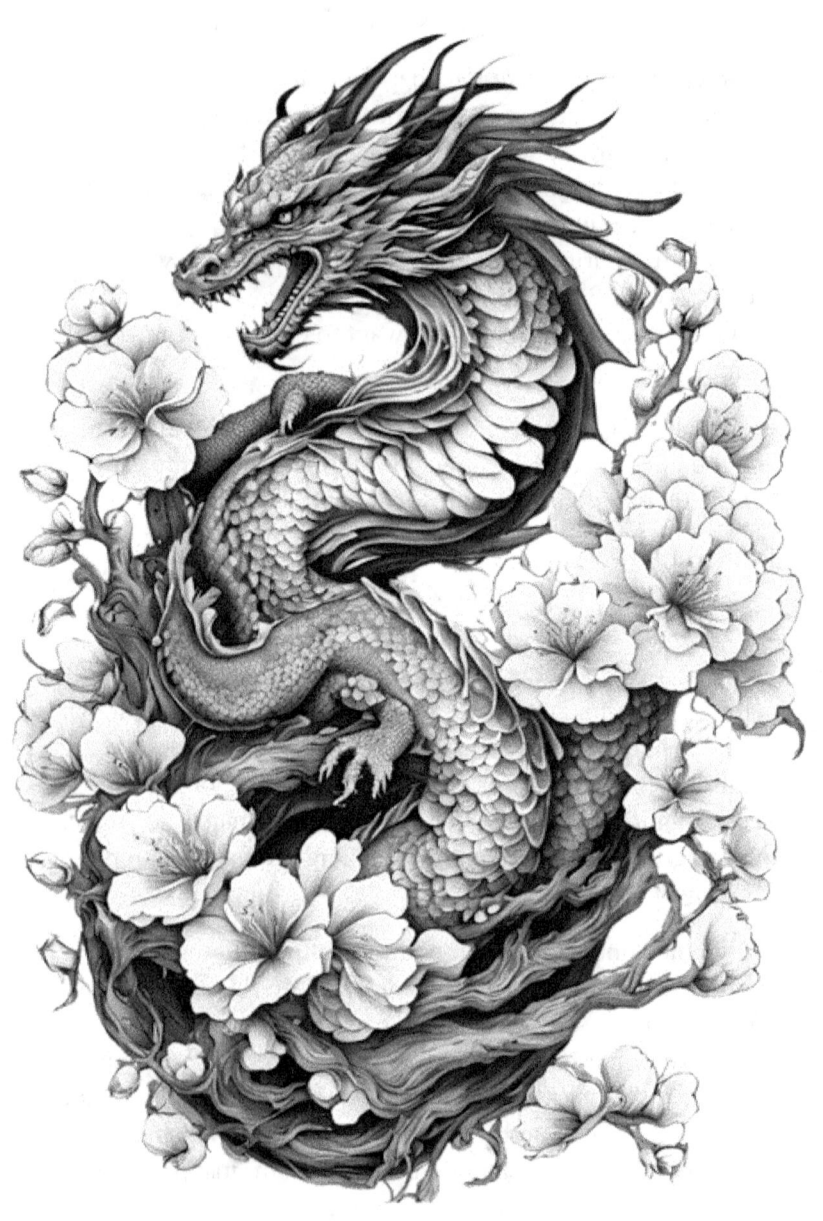

A floral dragon tattoo design

2. Protection

In many myths, dragons are seen as protectors. In Chinese culture, the dragon is a guardian of temples and sacred spaces, embodying divine protection and the safeguarding of treasures. Similarly, in European legends, dragons are often depicted guarding their hoards, reinforcing the idea of protection and vigilance.

A dragon tattoo can symbolize a person's protective nature, whether it be towards loved ones, personal values, or their own sense of identity. The image of a dragon standing guard can represent someone's commitment to safeguarding what they hold dear, showcasing loyalty and vigilance.

3. Wisdom

While dragons are often feared for their sheer might and power, they are also seen as wise, ancient beings with deep knowledge of the world. In various mythology, dragons are considered wise and benevolent protectors of the heavens, with an understanding of the cosmic order. In other cultures, dragons are depicted as ancient creatures who have lived through centuries, accumulating knowledge and experience.

A dragon tattoo can symbolize wisdom and a deep understanding of life's complexities. It can represent the wearer's quest for knowledge, both of themselves and the world around them. For those who value wisdom and intelligence, a dragon tattoo can reflect the idea of learning from the past and using that wisdom to navigate the present.

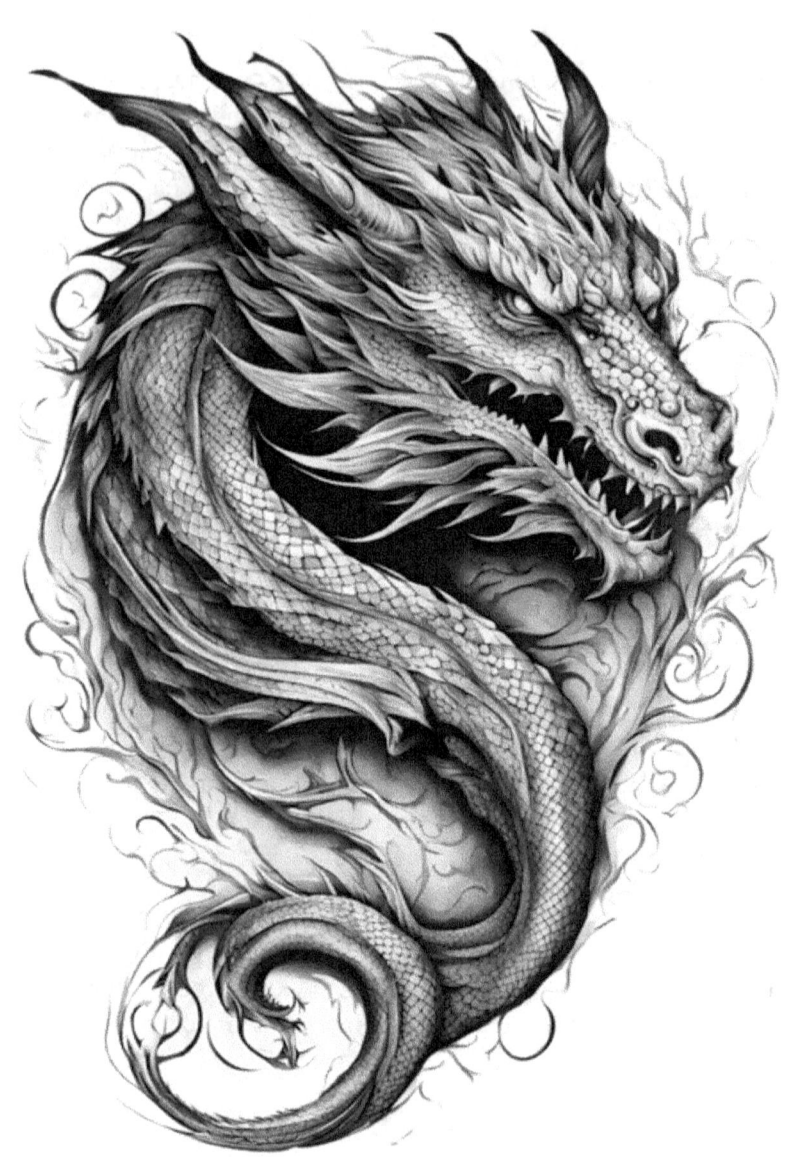

A mythical tattoo of a dragon

Phoenix: Rebirth, Transformation, Immortality

1. Rebirth

The phoenix is one of the most powerful symbols of rebirth and renewal, rising from its ashes to begin anew. This mythical bird is said to perish in flames only to be reborn from the ashes, representing the cycle of death and rebirth. In various mythologies, the phoenix is seen as a symbol of hope, renewal, and the continuous process of transformation.

People who choose phoenix tattoos often do so to represent personal renewal and the ability to rise from the ashes of old times they wish to improve on or forget. It can be a powerful symbol of recovery after a period of difficulty, loss, or change. A phoenix tattoo can signify that no matter how hard life gets, there is always the opportunity for rebirth and a fresh start.

2. Transformation

Transformation is another crucial theme in the mythology of the phoenix. Its extraordinary ability to change form through the process of death and rebirth signifies the idea of personal improvement and development. A phoenix tattoo can reflect someone's fundamental journey of self-transformation, highlighting their incredible capacity to change, grow, and become better over time. Whether it's a shift in perspective, career, or relationship, a phoenix tattoo can signify a visual symbol of that transformation. It celebrates the beauty of change, the strength in renewal, and the inherent power of overcoming hard times.

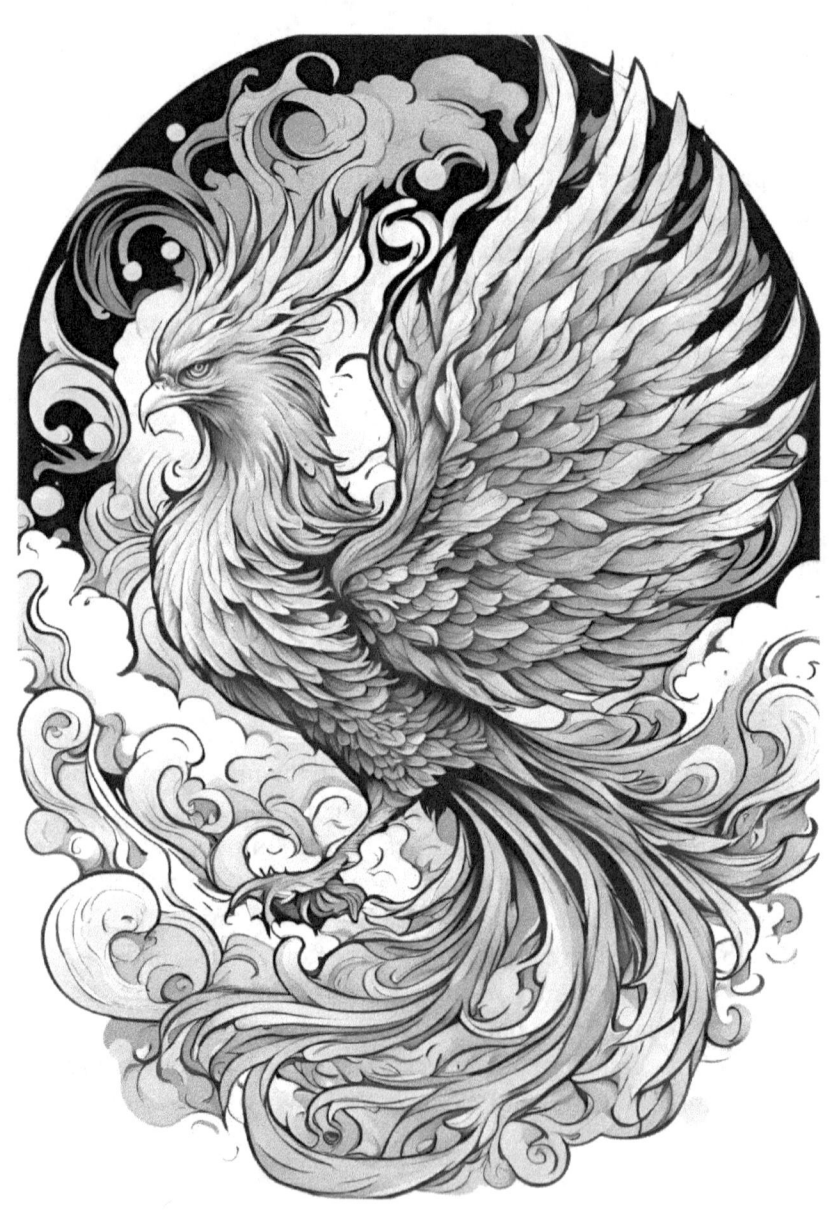

A phoenix tattoo design

3. Immortality

Beyond the concept of rebirth, the phoenix captures immortality through its eternal cycle of renewal. This mythical bird's remarkable ability to rise from its ashes represents a profound symbol of everlasting life and the perpetual rhythm of existence. Consequently, a phoenix tattoo signifies resilience, empowerment, and an ideology that the spirit transcends time. For many, a phoenix tattoo embodies the ethos of leaving a lasting mark on the world. It personifies the belief that, even in death, one's impact persists through actions, cherished memories, and the enduring spirit. This powerful imagery inspires hope and courage.

Unicorn: Purity, Innocence, Strength of Spirit

1. Purity

The unicorn, an extraordinary figure in numerous mythologies, exudes an aura of purity and innocence. Often envisioned as a majestic horse with a single spiraling horn, the unicorn symbolizes beauty, grace, and an unattainable ideal of purity. According to medieval European tales, only a genuinely virtuous individual could capture the elusive unicorn. A unicorn tattoo embodies a connection to purity of heart and spirit. It reflects a commitment to moral integrity, honesty, and the aspiration to live authentically, untouched by negativity. Seen as rare and untamed, unicorns represent precious ideals, inspiring individuals to protect and cherish them with reverence and dedication.

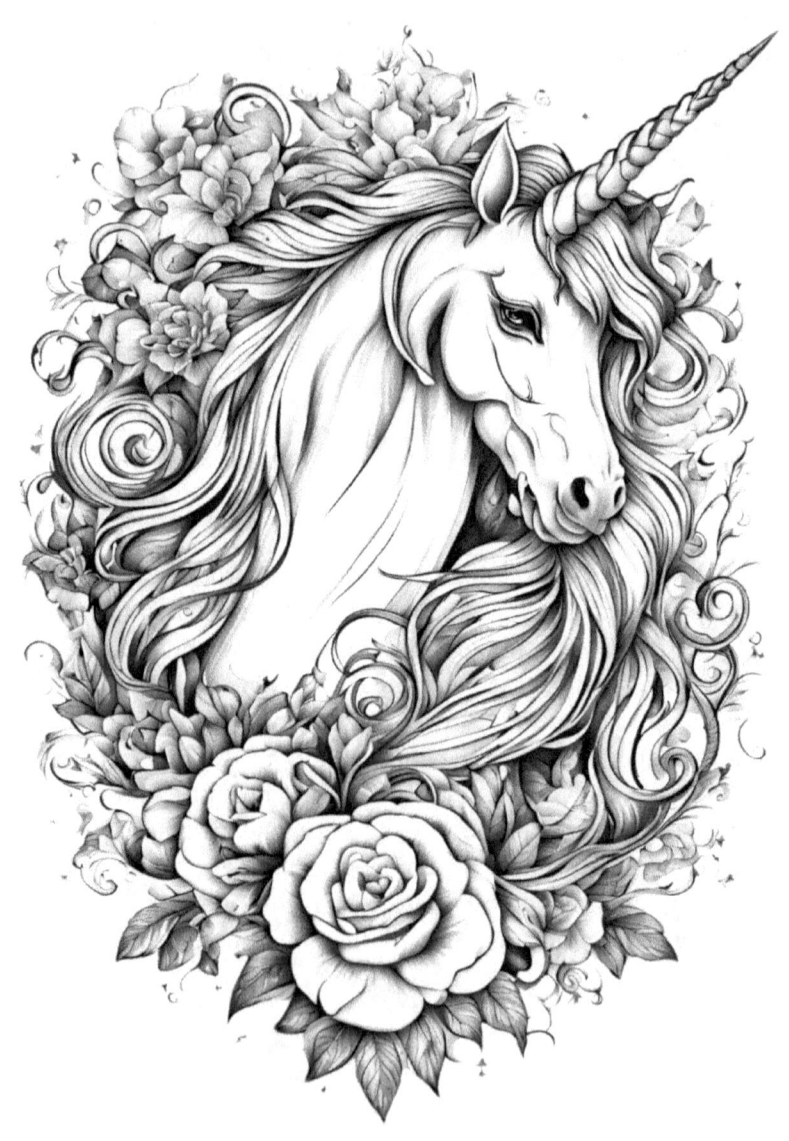

A unicorn tattoo design

2. Innocence

Unicorns embody the essence of innocence and wonder, captivating our imagination through art and storytelling. Their gentle and peaceful nature symbolizes a purity that remains unscathed by the world's harsh realities. A unicorn tattoo represents a profound commitment to preserving this inner innocence and wonder. It serves as a reminder to cherish life's simple joys and cultivate an open heart. These tattoos can teach us to hold onto joy, curiosity, and creativity. For those who cherish these qualities, a unicorn tattoo becomes a meaningful emblem of simplicity and purity, inspiring them to recognize and embrace the magic in everyday life. Each time they see the tattoo, they are reminded of the beauty that innocence brings to our existence.

3. Strength of Spirit

Though often seen as symbols of purity and innocence, unicorns are remarkable creatures of good luck and magic. Their gentle appearance conceals a fierce spirit, capable of defending themselves and others with the might of their iconic horn. This extraordinary blend of purity and magic makes the unicorn a compelling symbol of elegance and spiritual positivity. A unicorn tattoo can signify the embodiment of a strong spirit deeply rooted in kindness, integrity, and unwavering resolve. For those who value character and capability, the unicorn stands as a striking representation of the incredible freedom that arises from being true to oneself. With a unicorn tattoo, one not only celebrates beauty but also acknowledges the fortitude that resides within, making a statement of fearlessness and authenticity.

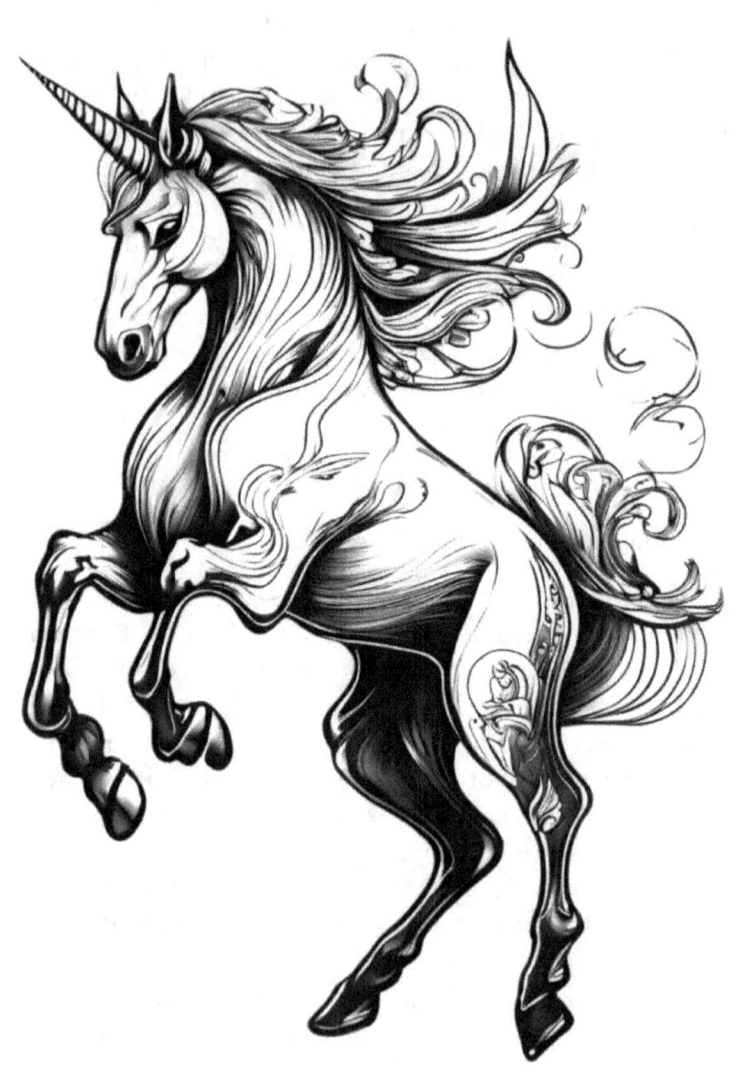

A unicorn tattoo design

Griffins: Courage, Honor, Guarding

1. Courage

The griffin, a mythical creature with the body of a lion and the wings and head of an eagle, has long been a symbol of courage and bravery. As a blend of the king of beasts (the lion) and the king of birds (the eagle), the griffin embodies competency and dominance in both land and sky. In ancient mythology, griffins were often depicted as protectors of treasure and sacred places, highlighting their role as valiant and noble guardians. A griffin tattoo can symbolize a person's loyalty, courage and generosity. It represents bravery and the ability to stand unwaveringly for one's beliefs. The griffin's fierce and noble demeanor reflects a strong-willed nature, the determination to protect oneself and others, and an enduring spirit that inspires confidence and honor.

2. Honor

Griffins are also associated with honor and loyalty, often depicted as guardians of sacred sites and treasures. In ancient mythology, griffins were believed to protect the gold of the gods and the tombs of kings, symbolizing their crucial role as protectors of what is most valuable. For individuals who value honor and integrity, a griffin tattoo can represent a steadfast commitment to living a life guided by these principles. It reflects a core sense of responsibility, duty, and loyalty to uphold one's values, protect what is sacred—whether family, beliefs or a way of life—and cultivate a legacy of honor that continues through generations. This fascinating mythical creature makes for a less common tattoo design.

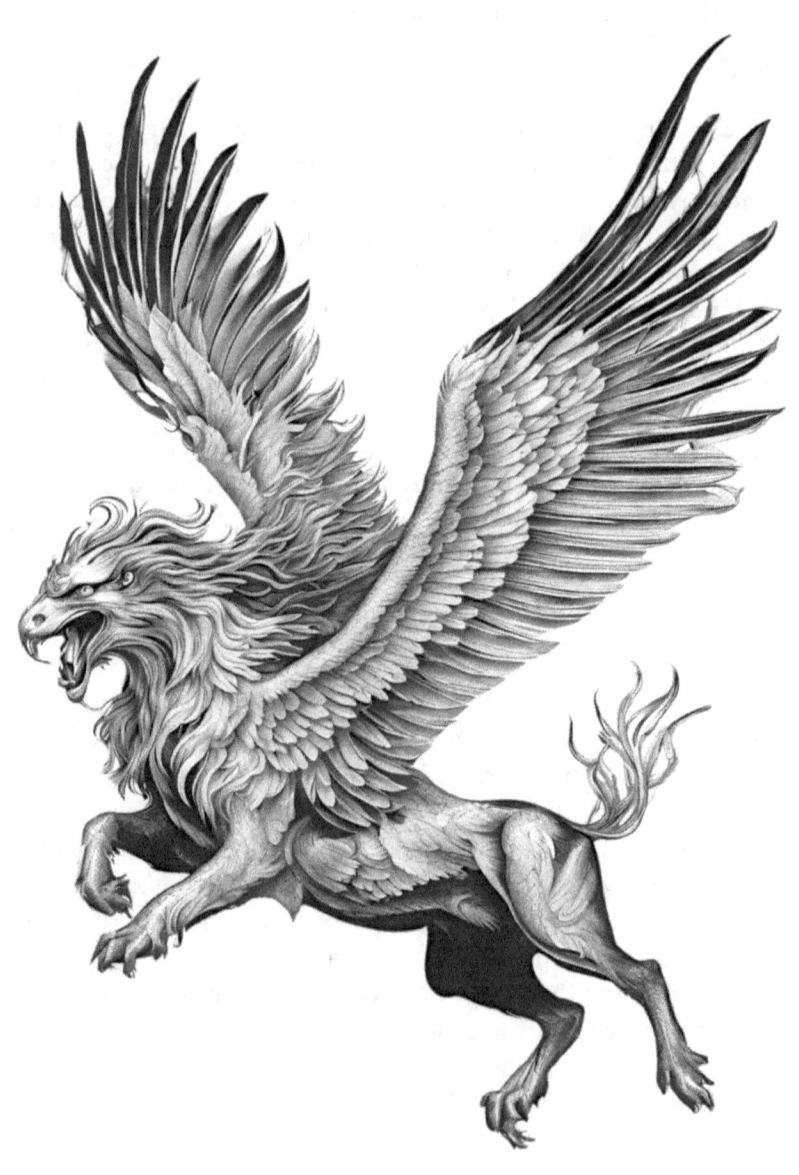

A griffin tattoo design

3. Guarding

Throughout mythology and history, griffins have been revered as fierce guardians, often depicted standing watch over valuable treasures or sacred possessions. Their dual nature makes them both formidable protectors and watchful sentinels. This unique blend of characteristics embodies essential qualities such as watchfulness, defense, and nobility. It symbolizes an individual's protective nature, reflecting their commitment to safeguarding loved ones, personal values, or even their own identity. Those who resonate with the griffin find inspiration in its image; They can represent loyalty and determination to defend what truly matters in their lives. The griffin's association with vigilance speaks to a deeper understanding of the world around us. It encourages individuals to remain observant and aware, ready to confront dangers that may arise. By adopting the griffin as a personal sign, one can embrace the essence of standing firm against dangers, illustrating a readiness to confront threats and overcome obstacles.

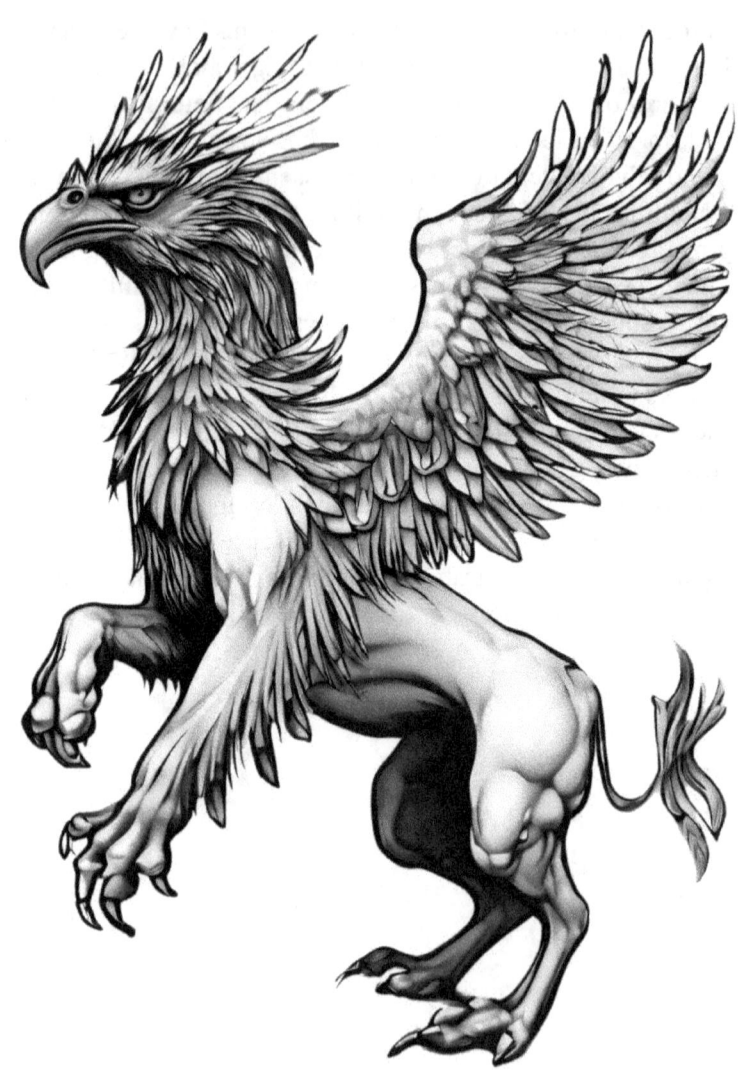

A griffin tattoo design

Fairies: Magic, Innocence, Freedom

Fairies, as enchanting figures of folklore, capture the essence of magic, innocence, and freedom. Their presence in various mythologies around the world has allowed them to become universal symbols, resonating with people of all backgrounds and beliefs. Each fairy tattoo tells a story that transcends time and space, inviting wearers to embody the enchanting qualities associated with these mystical beings

1. Magic

The allure of fairies lies in their underlying connection to the magical realm. Often portrayed with delicate wings and a radiant glow, fairies represent the unseen forces of nature and the wonder that exists in everyday life. They are typically seen as intermediaries between the human world and the mystical, embodying the idea that magic is not just an abstraction but also an integral part of our existence. Tattoos depicting fairies signify the enchantment in life. They encourage wearers to recognize and embrace the small wonders that surround them, fostering a profound sense of joy, creativity, and purpose. Many people choose fairy tattoos during mystical life events, symbolizing their desire to invite more magic and spontaneity into their lives.

Symbolism of Magic in Fairy Tattoos:

Manifestation of Dreams: Fairies often represent the idea of dreams coming to fruition. A fairy tattoo can symbolize a commitment to pursuing one's dreams and aspirations, constantly reminding the wearer that magical dreams can happen when they believe in themselves.

Connection to Nature: Many fairy designs incorporate elements of nature, such as vibrant flowers, ancient trees, and twinkling stars.

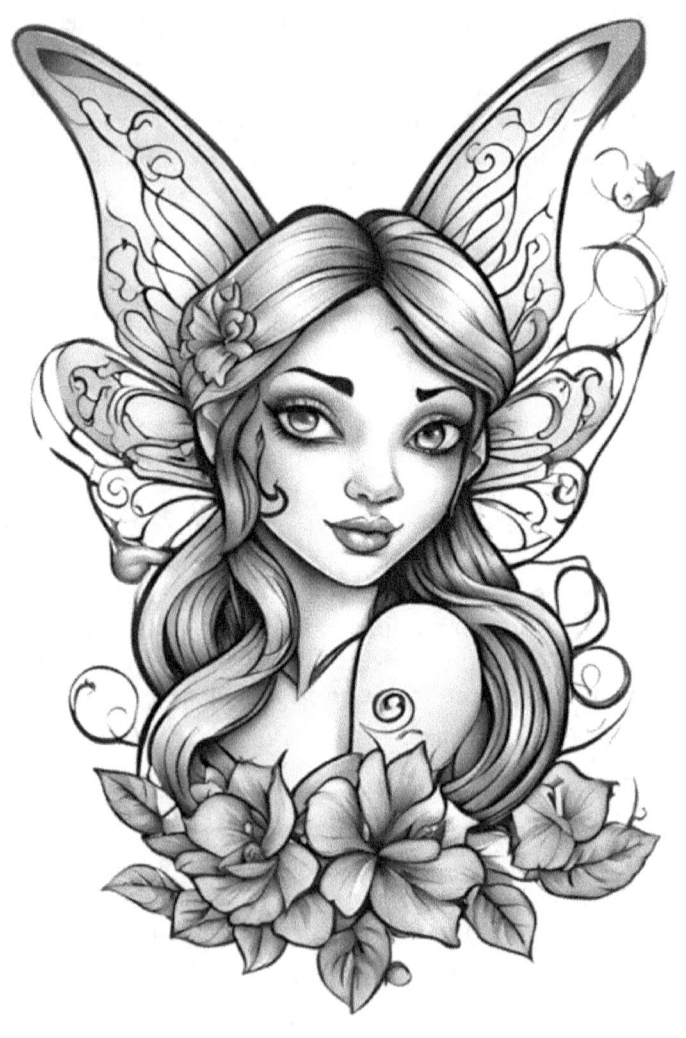

A fairy tattoo design

2. Innocence

Fairies are often depicted as innocent and playful beings, embodying a sense of wonder and joyousness. This association with innocence makes them a popular choice for tattoos that celebrate purity, creativity, and the beauty of life's simple pleasures. Fairies evoke a sense of magical freedom, reminding us of the carefree days of childhood and the importance of maintaining that sense of wonder as we grow older.
Fairy tattoos can represent an approach to life with curiosity and openness, allowing oneself to experience joy without the burdens of adult concerns.

For many, fairy tattoos represent cherished memories of childhood stories and fantasies. These elements add a personal touch, connecting wearers to their past and the memories they wish to retain. The playful nature of fairies encourages wearers to embrace their inner child. A fairy tattoo can symbolize the importance of play and laughter, reminding individuals to find joy in life's little moments.

3. Freedom

Fairies are often depicted as free spirits, unbound by the constraints of the mundane world. Their ability to fly from flower to flower, dance in moonlit glades, and soar through the skies embodies the essence of freedom. This connection encourages individuals to find freedom in the great outdoors, celebrating the beauty and tranquility found in natural surroundings. For many, a fairy tattoo signifies a longing for liberation, self-expression, and the ability to live life freely. Fairy tattoos can symbolize the wearer's journey toward personal liberation and self-acceptance. They serve as a constant reminder to pursue passions and dreams without fear of judgment or limitations.

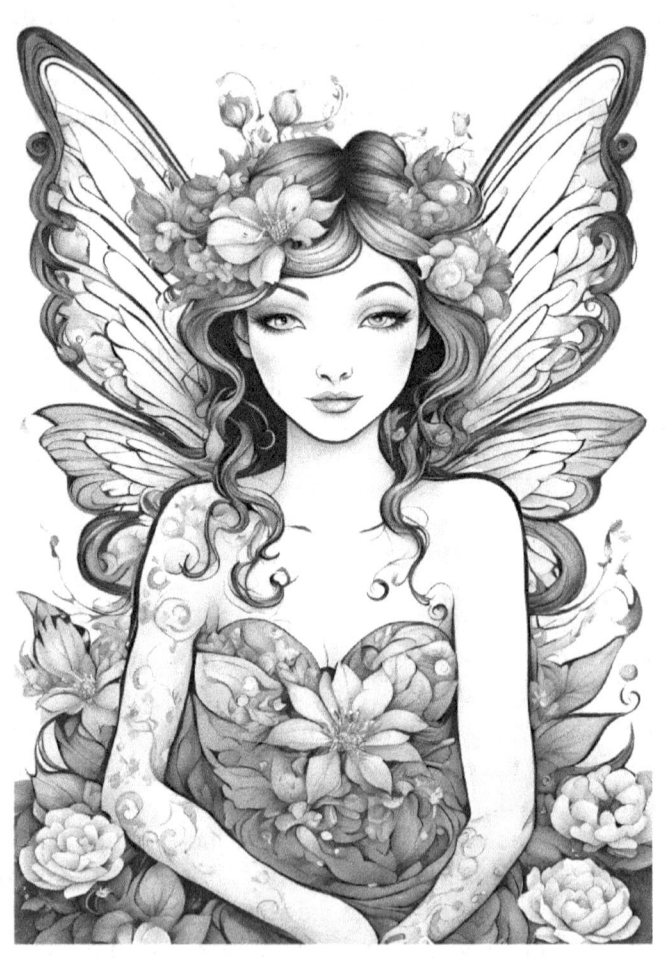

A fairy tattoo design

Chapter Conclusion

Every legendary magical being comes with a deep-rooted background and cultural value, making the choice to get a tattoo an important moment for introspection and storytelling. By delving into the meanings associated with these symbols, people can select designs that align with their stories and feelings. As individuals wear these enchanting creatures as tattoos, they not only honor the beauty of creativity but also welcome a sense of wonder, power, and liberation into their lives. From the renewal represented by a phoenix to the elegance of a unicorn or the bravery of a griffin, tattoos of mythical beings showcase the incredible traits that may lie within each of us. Embrace your selected fantastical creature and allow its meaning to inspire and guide you. Invite that enchantment into your daily existence and celebrate the transformation it offers.

Chapter 5: symbolism of the human body in tattoos

Tattoos featuring human body elements often delve into profound themes, exploring the relationship between physical forms and the bottom-line meanings they portray. These designs represent not only aesthetic expressions but also vision, power, love, mortality, and identity. The human body has long been a canvas for expressing strong meanings, and when it comes to tattoos, different parts of the body carry compelling symbolic weight. Tattoos of eyes, hands, hearts, skulls, and portraits speak to universal human experiences, visions, power, and even mortality. These tattoos explore timeless themes, allowing the wearer to express individual truths and philosophies through meaningful imagery. In this chapter, we explore how different parts of the human body are represented in tattoo art and the various symbolism they carry.

Eyes: Vision, Intuition, Protection

The eye has been a important symbol across various cultures and spiritual traditions, often representing vision, knowledge, and insight. Eye tattoos can carry numerous meanings depending on how they are depicted, ranging from protection to intuition.

Symbolism and Meaning

Vision and Perception: The eye is often associated with the idea of seeing beyond the surface. A tattoo of an eye can symbolize clarity of vision—both literal and metaphorical—suggesting that the wearer values truth and seeks to uncover hidden meanings in life.

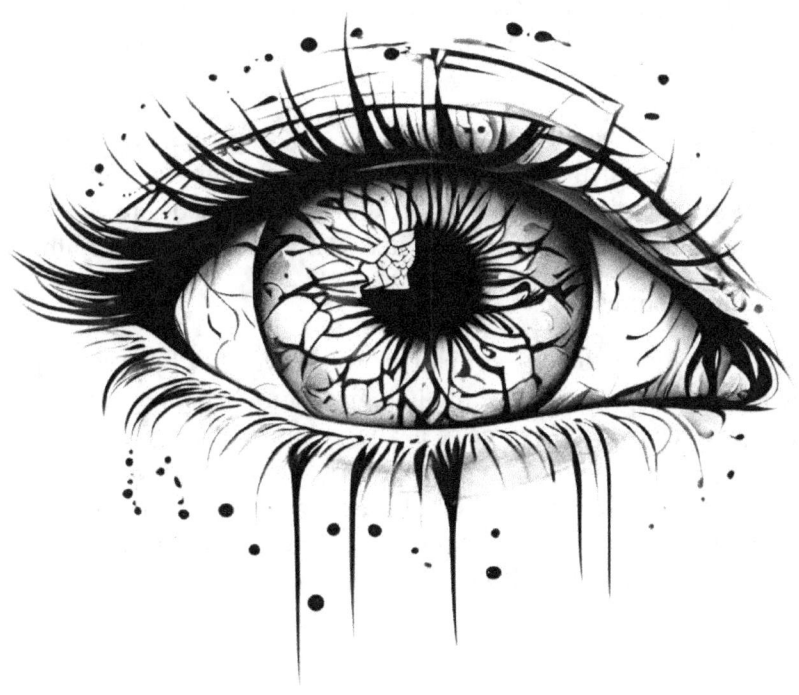

An eye tattoo design

Intuition: In many cultures, the eye is seen as a symbol of wisdom and intuition. A tattoo of a single eye, often referred to as the "third eye," can symbolize heightened awareness and a deeper connection to one's own instincts and understanding of the world.

Protection: The "Evil Eye" tattoo is one of the most well-known protective symbols, believed to ward off negative energy or ill-will from others. This design often features a stylized eye surrounded by vivid colors, acting as a talisman that shields the wearer from harm.

Omniscience: The idea of an all-seeing eye, often positioned in mystical symbolism, reflects the concept of omnipresence or an all-knowing entity. When tattooed, it may convey a desire to maintain awareness of both the outer world and one's inner truth.

Cultural Interpretations

In ancient times, the "Eye of Horus" was a symbol of protection, health, and restoration. The mythological story behind it depicts the eye as a powerful source of healing. Similarly, in other mytholgy, the "Evil Eye" represents protection from envy and malevolence. These rich cultural meanings make eye tattoos a versatile and deeply personal form of expression, whether they are chosen for spiritual protection or as a mark of inner awareness.

Hands: Power, Creation, Connection

Hands are one of the most dynamic symbols in tattoo art, representing a wide range of concepts such as creation, power, and human connection. Hands are literally and metaphorically tools of expression, and tattoos that feature hands often carry themes of agency, interaction, and mastery over one's environment.

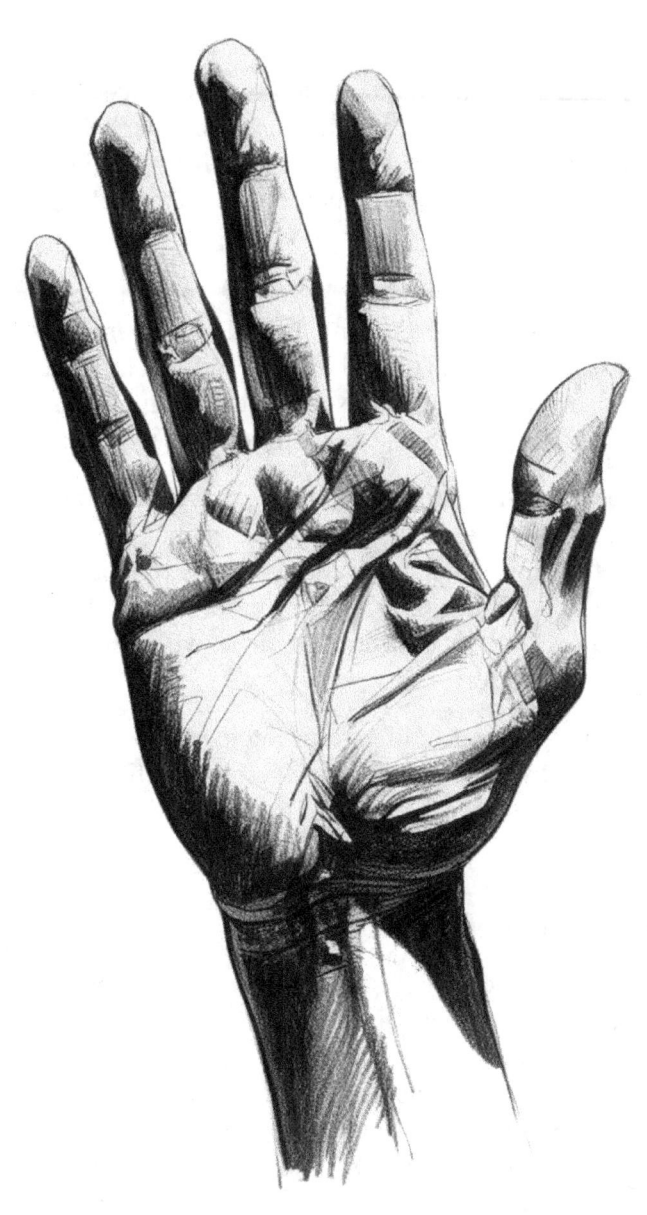

A standard hand drawing design

Symbolism and Meaning

Power and Control: A tattoo of a raised or clenched fist symbolizes force, unity, and defiance. This symbol has been historically associated with movements for social justice and personal empowerment, embodying the idea of taking control over one's destiny.

Creation and Craftsmanship: Tattoos featuring hands engaged in creative work, such as drawing, holding tools, or playing instruments, emphasize the importance of creativity and craftsmanship in the wearer's life. It can signify a person's pride in their artistic or professional abilities.

Connection and Compassion: Hand tattoos that show two hands reaching out or clasping together often symbolize human connection, love, and unity. These designs can represent relationships, partnerships, and the bond shared between people. They can also serve as a tribute to those who offer guidance, support, or comfort.

Spiritual Significance: In various interpretations, hands symbolize divine guidance or intervention, reflecting the belief that higher powers can offer support, protection, and direction.

Historical and Cultural Meaning

Throughout history, hands have played significant roles in different cultures. For example, the "Hamsa" hand is a popular universal symbol, used as an amulet to protect against harm and bring good fortune. The symbolism of hands transcends culture and time, making them a powerful motif in tattoo art, representing both practical and symbolic notions of power, control, and connection.

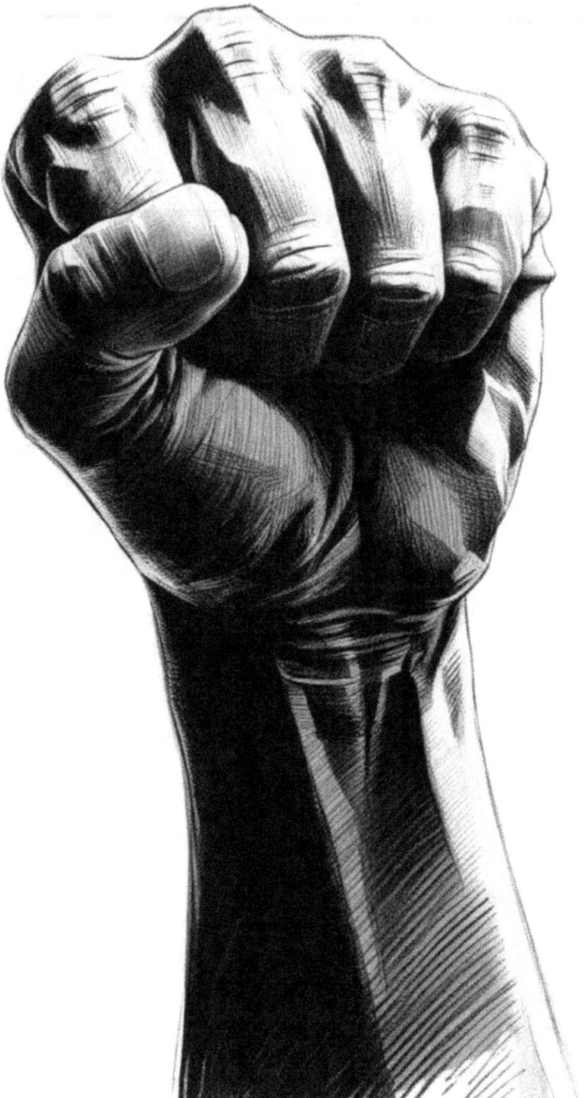

A clenched fist design

Hearts: Love, Compassion, Courage

The heart is perhaps the most universally recognized symbol of love and lust. Heart tattoos, however, go beyond the simple association with romance. They can embody a range of human emotions, from compassion and kindness to the loss of a loved one.

Symbolism and Meaning

Love and Affection: The classic heart shape is synonymous with love, whether it's romantic, familial, or self-love. People often get heart tattoos as a way of expressing affection for loved ones or to celebrate meaningful connections.

Courage and Strength: In certain contexts, the heart represents courage—like the phrase "having heart" in times of despair. A tattoo featuring a heart can symbolize bravery.

Compassion and Kindness: A tattoo of a heart, especially when paired with elements like flowers or ribbons, can signify a person's compassion for nature. It serves as a reminder of the importance of kindness, empathy, and understanding in their life.

Personal Loss and Tribute: Broken heart tattoos or hearts pierced with arrows or daggers are often used to signify grief, heartbreak, or loss. These designs can act as memorials to lost loved ones or as symbols of emotional pain that the wearer has endured.

Cultural Significance

In numerous cultures, the heart is regarded as the center of emotion and the essence of life. Modern heart tattoos can embody a wide array of personal meanings, signifying everything from commemorating cherished relationships to marking emotional times. For many, these tattoos remind one of love, resilience, and the intricate stories that shape their lives.

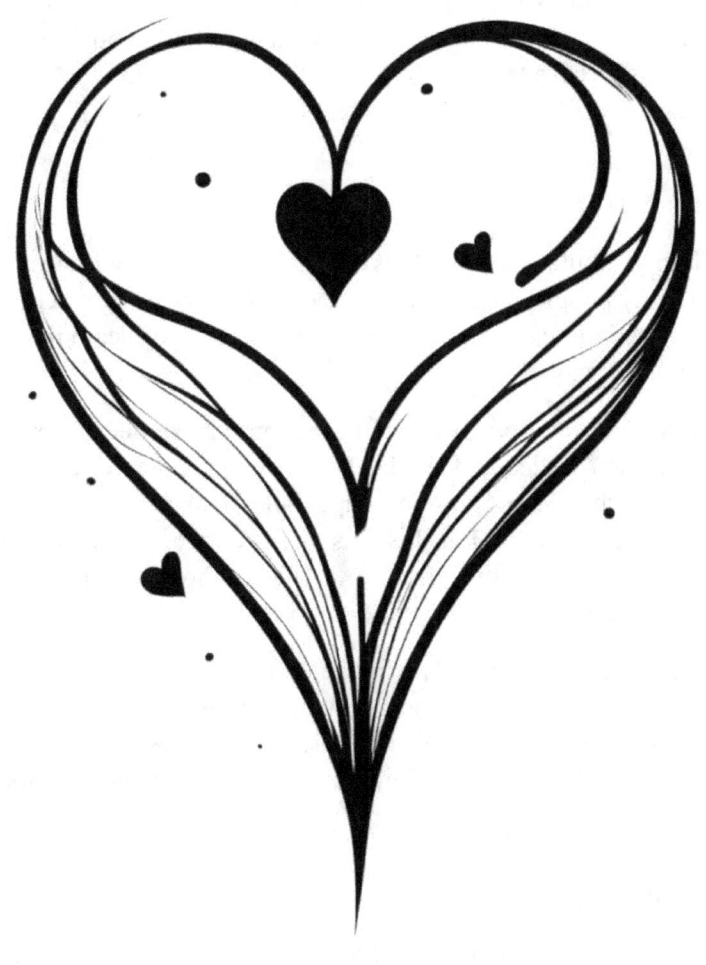

A simple heart tattoo design

Skeletons and Skulls: Mortality, Rebirth, Legacy

Skeletons and skulls are some of the most powerful and popular symbols in tattoo art, often representing mortality, death, and the legacies we leave behind. While they may initially appear grim or macabre, these tattoos carry a rich depth of meaning, addressing life's impermanence and temporary nature of existence.

Symbolism and Meaning

Mortality: Skulls and skeletons are often associated with loss of life. Many people choose skull tattoos to embrace the idea that life is fleeting, and to reflect on the inevitability of death in a meaningful way.

Legacy and Memory: Skulls and skeletons can serve as symbols of the legacy we leave behind. They remind the wearer that although life is temporary, the impact they make can endure beyond their lifetime. For this reason, many people choose these designs to represent the lasting influence of those they have loved or admired.

Rebellion and Defiance: The image of a skull is also tied to the idea of rebellion, often associated with the refusal to conform or the rejection of societal expectations. Skull tattoos have long been favored by people that embrace defiance and individualism.

Cultural Interpretations

Skulls are also prominent in pirate folklore, symbolizing danger, adventure, and fearlessness. These diverse interpretations make skull tattoos a dynamic and meaningful choice, offering both a reflection on mortality and a celebration of life.

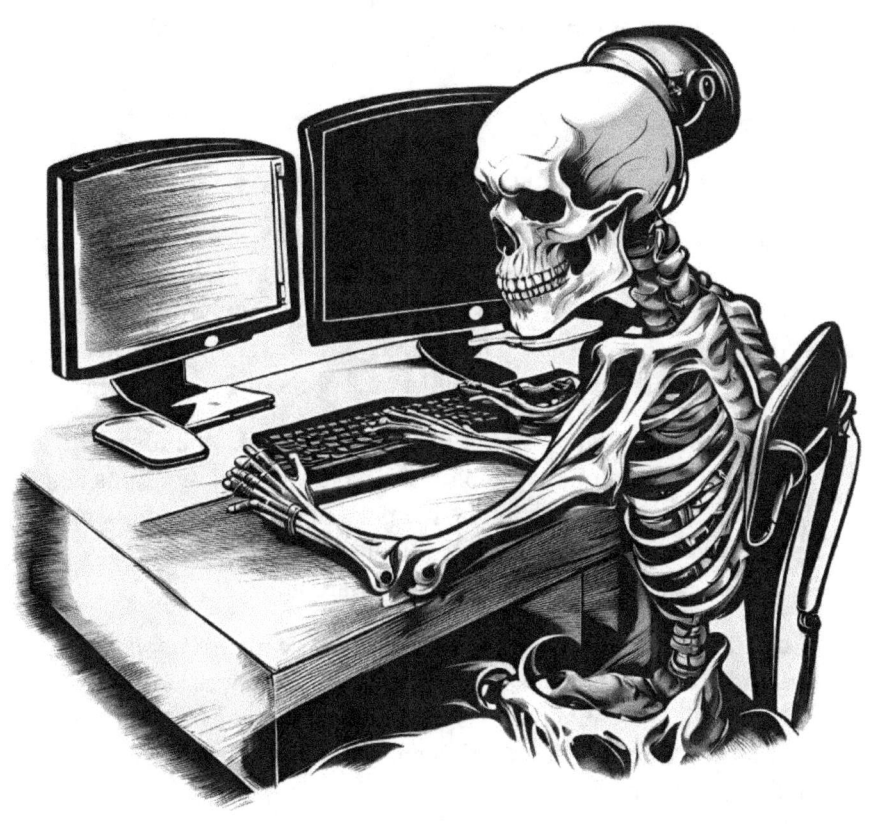

A conceptual skeleton at a desk tattoo design

Faces and Portraits: Identity, Memory, Tribute

Portrait tattoos, whether they depict the faces of loved ones, celebrities, or abstract figures, are a deeply personal form of body art. These tattoos often carry significant emotional weight, symbolizing memory, identity, or tribute to someone who has impacted the wearer's life.

Symbolism and Meaning

Identity: A portrait tattoo can be a powerful expression of personal identity. Some people choose to tattoo their own portrait or a stylized version of themselves, using body art to reflect their sense of self. Others may opt for abstract or surreal portraits that reflect one's feelings or aspects of their personality.

Memory and Tribute: Memorial tattoos often take the form of portraits of loved ones who have passed away. These tattoos act as living tributes, honoring the memory of someone significant in the wearer's life. The detailed likeness can represent a way to keep that person close, even after they are gone.

Admiration and Inspiration: Portrait tattoos can also depict individuals who have inspired or influenced the wearer in a meaningful way. Whether it's an artist, activist, or personal hero, these tattoos express admiration and the impact that person has had on the wearer's worldview.

Emotional Depth: Faces are deeply expressive, and tattoos that feature emotional or dramatic facial expressions can convey complex feelings. These designs can represent everything from joy and sorrow to anger or contemplation, allowing the wearer to externalize their inner emotional feelings.

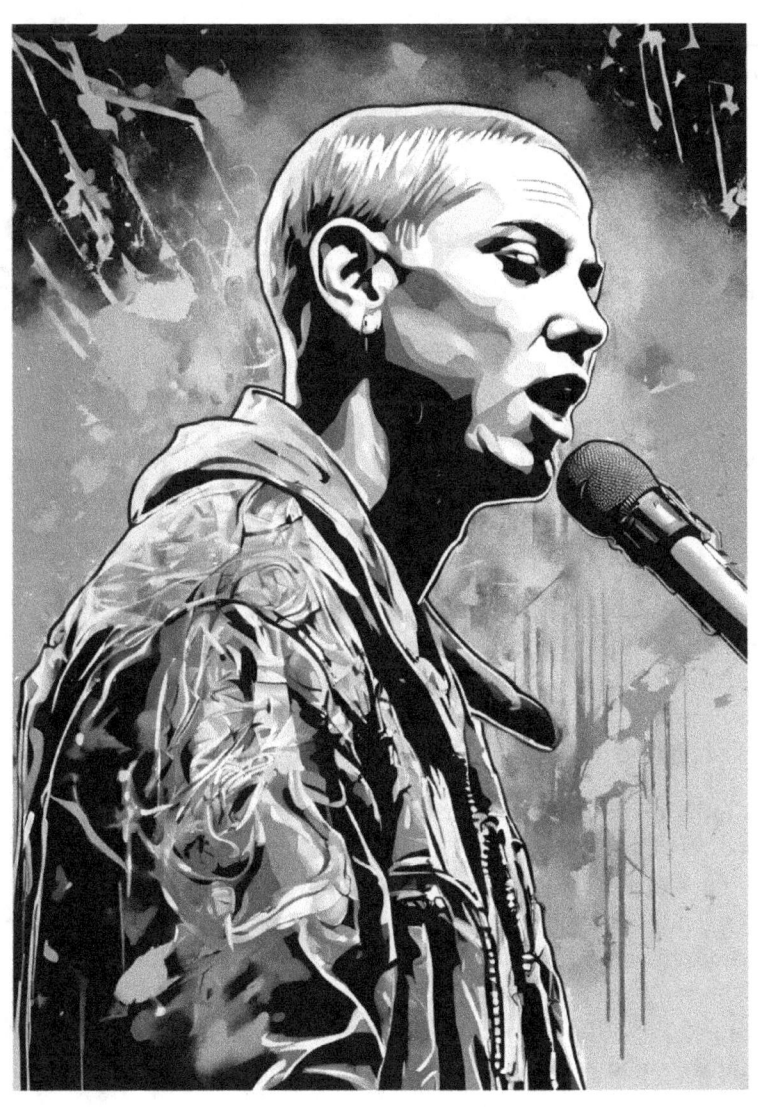

A conceptual portrait tattoo design

Cultural and Artistic interpretation

Portrait tattoos are a form of art that requires great skill and precision, often resembling realistic or hyper-realistic styles. They offer a way to remember someone, capturing their likeness in a way that will last a lifetime. For many, portrait tattoos are the ultimate form of tribute, displaying a person's legacy.

Conclusion

In conclusion, tattoos featuring different parts of the human body—whether eyes, hands, hearts, skulls, or portraits—represent universal themes of life, identity, love, and mortality. These designs are not only aesthetically striking but carry layers of meaning that can enrich the wearer. The symbolism of the human body in tattoos offers a rich variety of meanings that resonate with ones past and cultural connections. From the insights of eye tattoos to the power of hands, the love represented by hearts, the contemplation of mortality in skeletons and skulls, and the tribute within faces and portraits, these motifs invite wearers to reflect on their life and embrace their identities.

As individuals choose tattoos that speak to their values and experiences, they create a visual narrative that celebrates the human story. Each tattoo signals the intricate relationship between the body and the meanings we attach to it, inviting us to explore the depths of our humanity through art. In this discovery of showing ones feelings, tattoos become more than mere designs; they transform into great symbols of who we are and what we stand for.

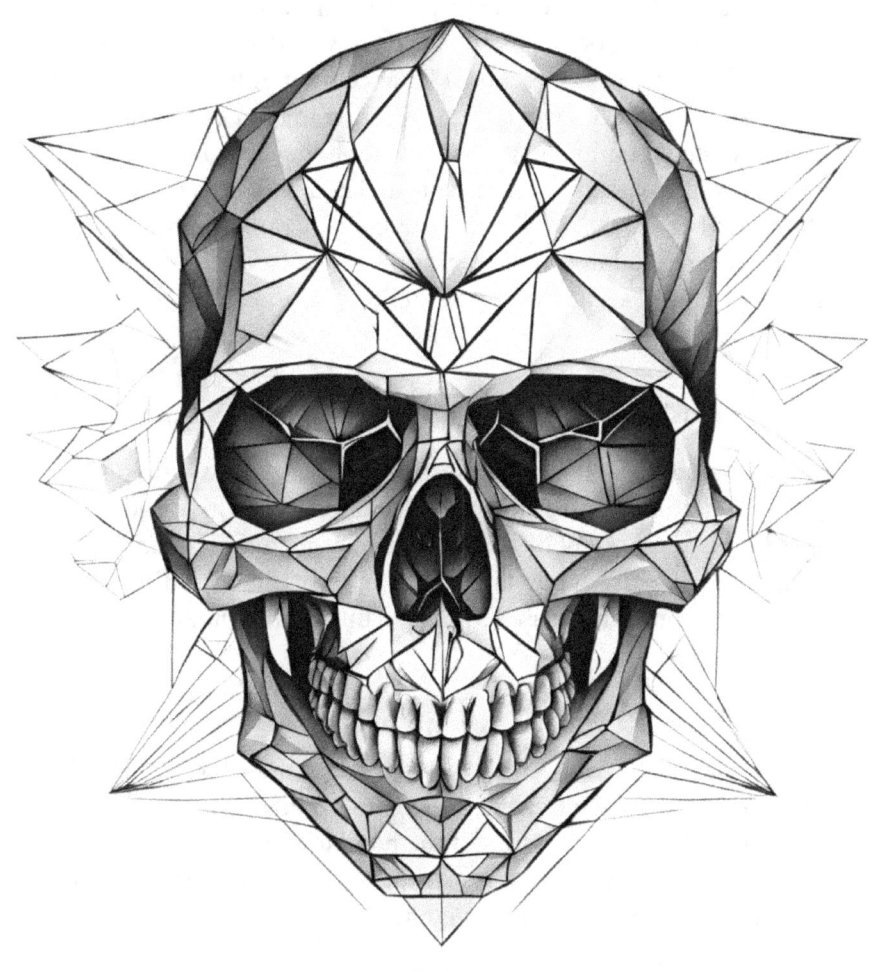

A skull tattoo design

Chapter 6: Spiritual and Philosophical Tattoos

Tattoos have long served as a medium for displaying spiritual and philosophical ideas. They can be a reflection of one's feelings, an exploration of identity, or a manifestation of values. Spiritual and philosophical tattoos have a vast depth, representing timeless concepts of balance, mortality, and energy. These tattoos offer the wearer a connection to their core beliefs or philosophical outlook. Whether symbolizing enlightenment, balance, or the passage of time, spiritual and philosophical tattoos are both meaningful and visually captivating. In this chapter, we delve into four meaningful symbols: the lotus, yin and yang, hourglass and infinity symbol.

Lotus: Flourishment, Enlightenment, Overcoming Obstacles

The lotus flower is one of the most peaceful and pure symbols in spiritual tattoo designs. Lotus tattoos embody deep love and open-heartedness, symbolizing profound transformation and radiant inner beauty. They highlight our ability to cherish meaningful connections and embrace vulnerability in all relationships.

Symbolism and Meaning

Flourishment: The lotus grows from muddy, murky water, which symbolizes the difficulties one can endure in life. The development from the bottom of the pond to the surface and the flower's ultimate bloom represents spiritual flourishment. A lotus tattoo can also symbolize love and new beginnings.

Enlightenment: In many spiritual traditions, the lotus represents enlightenment and purity of mind and spirit. The unfolding petals symbolize the expansion of consciousness and the journey toward greater wisdom and understanding.

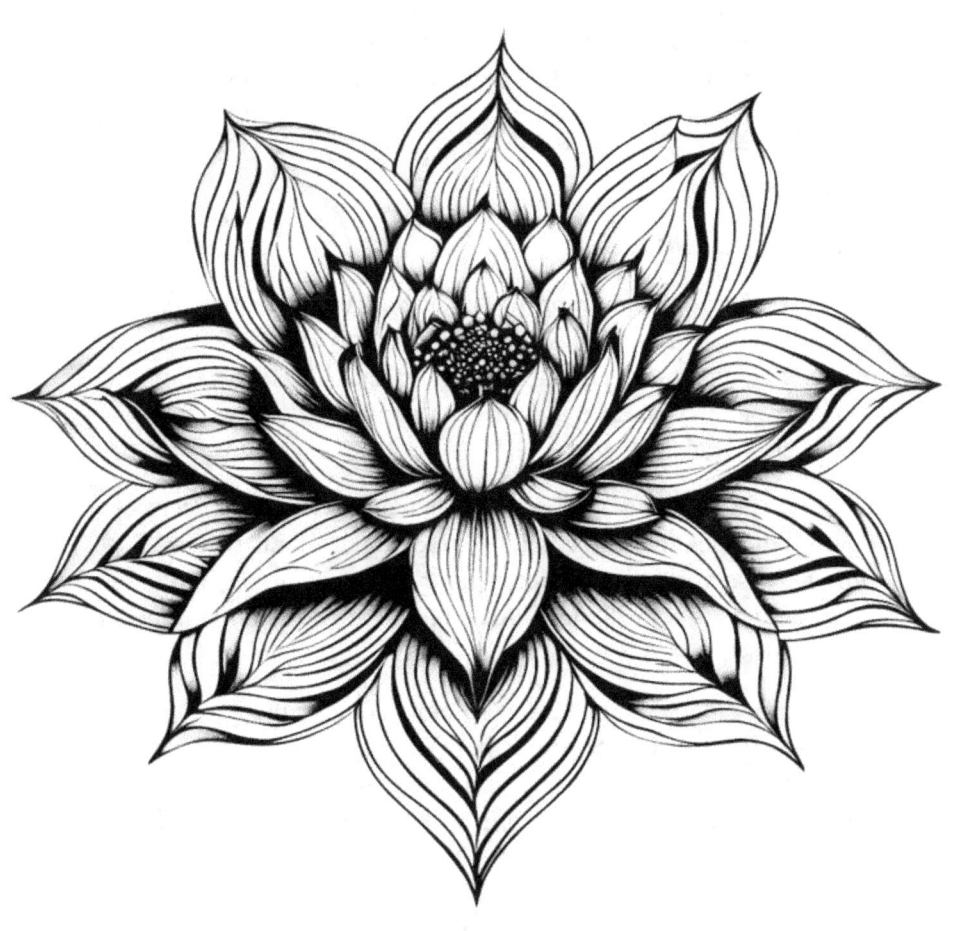

A lotus tattoo design

Yin and Yang: Balance, Harmony, Duality

The Yin and Yang symbol, originating from ancient Chinese philosophy, represents the concept of duality, balance, and harmony. It conveys the idea that opposing forces are interconnected and interdependent in the natural world, creating a delicate balance. This iconic black-and-white symbol has become a popular tattoo design, often used to present the need for balance in one's life or the understanding of life's inherent contrasts.

Symbolism and Meaning

Balance: Yin and Yang represent the balance between opposite forces—light and dark, male and female, activity and rest, etc. A Yin and Yang tattoo symbolizes the idea that life's opposing forces are interconnected and that harmony arises when these forces are in balance.

Duality: The Yin and Yang design also expresses the concept of duality, the idea that life contains opposing elements that are not only necessary but also complementary. For example, happiness cannot exist without sadness, and strength is defined by moments of weakness.

Harmony: Yin and Yang tattoos often symbolize the harmonious relationship between seemingly conflicting forces. The symbol indicates that harmony can be achieved even in times of chaos or tension, and that opposites often contribute to a greater whole.

In tattoo art, Yin and Yang symbols are often stylized or paired with other elements such as animals, plants, or geometric shapes to further emphasize balance and unity. This tattoo is popular for people seeking to display their philosophical views.

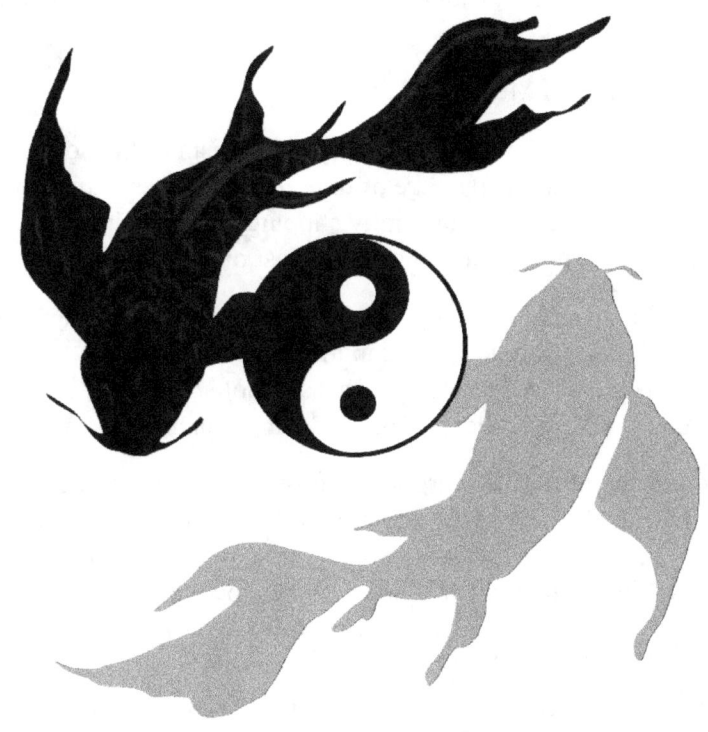

An example of Yin and Yang design with koi fish

Hourglass: The Passage of Time, Mortality, Impermanence

The hourglass is an iconic symbol of time and its fleeting nature. As the sand in the hourglass trickles down, it represents the unstoppable passage of time and the transient nature of our existence. Hourglass tattoos often reflect themes of mortality, the inevitability of death, and the importance of living fully in the present.

Symbolism and Meaning

The Passage of Time: The primary symbolism of the hourglass revolves around the passage of time. An hourglass tattoo can implicate that time is constantly slipping away, urging the wearer to live in the present and make the most of every moment.

Mortality: The hourglass is often associated with death and the inevitability of life's end. It can mean that death is an inescapable part of existence. This symbolism is often used in tattoos to prompt reflection on life's impermanence.

Impermanence: The hourglass's constant movement of sand represents the impermanence of all things. The tattoo can signify that everything in life is temporary, whether it be material possessions, relationships, or even one's own existence.

Cultural Interpretations

The hourglass has long been associated with the measurement of time, and its imagery has appeared in art, literature, and spiritual teachings. In some cultures, the hourglass is connected to the idea of fate and destiny, symbolizing how time shapes our experiences and outcomes. The hourglass is also linked to the concept of cyclicality, representing the eternal cycle of life, death, and rebirth.

In modern tattoo designs, the hourglass is often depicted with intricate details, such as skulls, flowers, or celestial elements, to further enhance its symbolism.

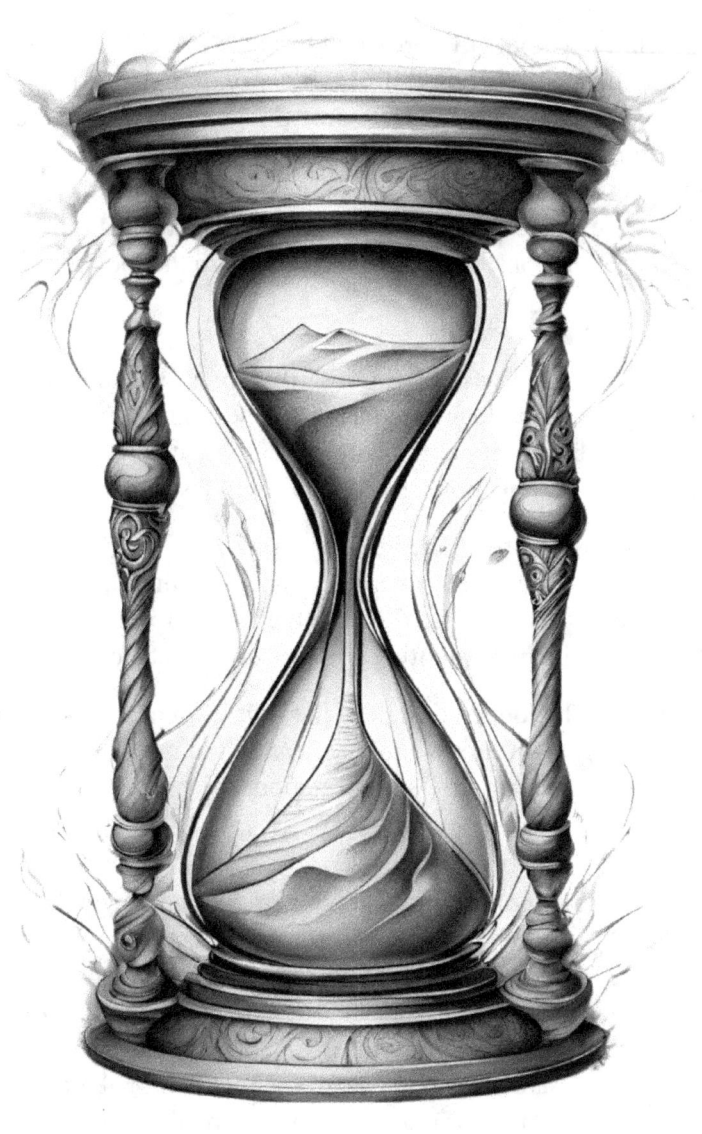

An hourglass tattoo design

Infinity Symbol: Eternity, Limitless Possibilities

The infinity symbol, a figure-eight turned on its side, represents eternity and limitless possibilities. It's a symbol of boundlessness, suggesting that some things—whether they be love, energy, or existence—are endless and beyond comprehension. Infinity tattoos are a popular choice for those seeking to express their belief in the infinite nature of the universe, a relationship or something close to the individual.

Symbolism and Meaning

Eternity: The infinity symbol primarily represents eternity, whether it's eternal love, friendship, or the continuous cycle of life and death. Infinity tattoos often signify that certain relationships, connections, or concepts will last forever.

Limitless Possibilities: The infinity symbol is also associated with the idea of limitless potential. It suggests that there are no boundaries or restrictions, allowing the wearer to show their belief in infinite opportunities or their continuous possibilities.

Continuity: The looped design of the infinity symbol reflects the continuous flow of life, without a clear beginning or end. This can be an indicator of life's interrelation.

Cultural Interpretations

The infinity symbol has roots in mathematics and metaphysical philosophy, where it is used to represent the concept of an unending continuum. However, its simplicity and elegance have made it a popular tattoo choice across different cultures. In some interpretations, it symbolizes the infinite nature of the soul. Infinity tattoos are often personalized with additional elements such as names, dates, or other meaningful symbols. The adaptability of the design makes it a versatile choice for those looking to show philosophies about eternity, endless possibilities, or the boundless nature of existence.

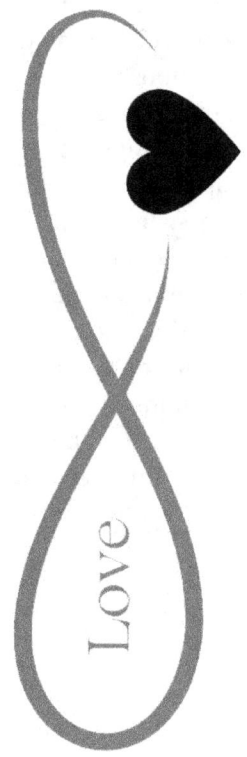

A simple infinity love design

Chapter Conclusion

Tattoos inspired by spiritual and philosophical concepts, such as the lotus flower or the infinity symbol, embody rich meanings tied to harmony, and the transient nature of existence. These body art pieces indicate life's profound teachings, fostering a connection to one's beliefs and dreams. Whether they signify enlightenment, emotional equilibrium, the flow of time, or energy alignment, these tattoos represent the spiritual and philosophical truths that influence our lives. Spiritual and philosophical tattoos provide significant channels for introspection. Each design, from the enlightening lotus to the harmonious yin and yang, captures distinct meanings. As individuals embrace these symbols, they embark on meaningful self-discovery, contemplation, and introspection paths. These tattoos invite wearers to delve into their values and encourage exploration of the intricacies of existence. By adorning their skin with these carefully chosen images, individuals create a visual narrative encompassing their thoughts. Ultimately, spiritual and philosophical tattoos transform into more than mere adornments; they become vital statements of identity, purpose, and understanding.

Chapter 7: Inspirational Words and Phrases

Tattoos have transformed from simple body decorations into meaningful declarations of self-identity, values, and philosophical displays. One of the most impactful methods to convey one's feelings, dreams, and memories is through empowering words. Tattoos embellished with phrases, quotations, and meaningful words provide a profoundly intimate form of self-identity. Unlike symbolic designs that may hold various interpretations, word-based tattoos deliver distinct messages, sentiments, or philosophies with clarity and intent. These inked thoughts can encapsulate personal ideologies, celebrate pivotal life events, or display essential virtues like Believe, Focus, or Freedom. The trend of using inspiring words and phrases for tattoos has surged in popularity, admired for their motivational traits and variety of design possibilities. From powerful single words that communicate meaningfully to elaborate phrases and personalized calligraphy, these tattoos can signify lasting declarations about what the individual values most. In this chapter, we will delve into various styles of word tattoos, including impactful single words and meaningful phrases.

Single Words: Hope, Strength, Courage, Freedom

Single-word tattoos often deliver profound sentiments or values in a minimalist yet striking manner. A solitary word etched onto the skin can show ambitions, thoughts, or guiding ideologies. These tattoos are not only easy to create, allowing for imaginative placement and typography, but they also transmit a clear and resounding message that can interpret moments of the wearer's past. Additionally, the simplicity of a single word allows it to be incorporated into broader themes or layered meanings, enhancing its emotional importance.

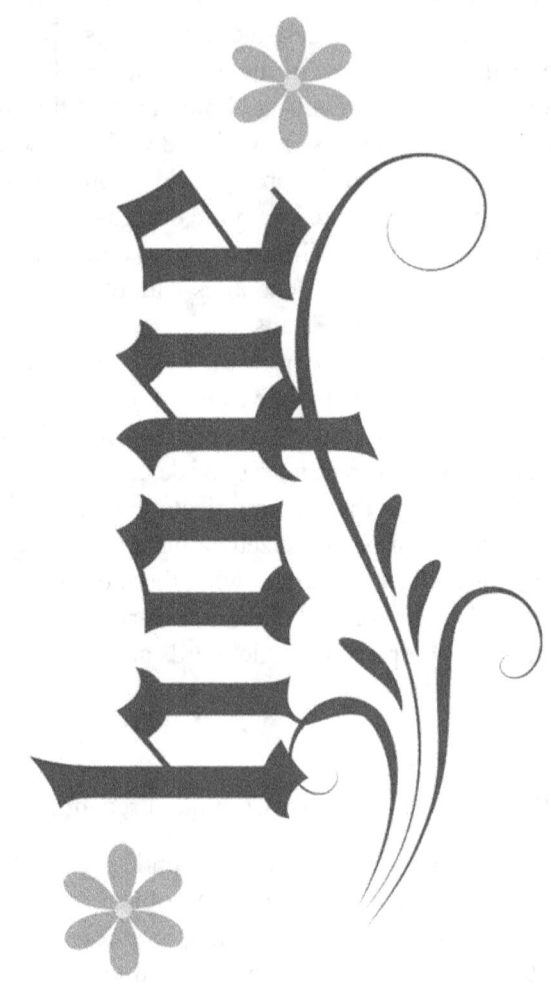

A single word 'hope' design

Hope

The word "Hope" is one of the most popular single-word tattoos, symbolizing unwavering optimism and faith in a brighter, more fulfilling future. Many individuals choose "Hope" as a tattoo after conquering personal struggles, using it as a constant signal to maintain a positive outlook and strive for better days ahead. This simple yet profound word carries a daily source of positive inspiration for the individuals that choose it. It holds the belief that, despite challenges, there remains the possibility for joy and renewal. Those who decide on a "Hope" tattoo often reflect on their past, recognizing the battles they've fought and the lessons learned. The tattoo becomes a piece of art and a testament to their strength and aspirations for a fulfilling life. Simple script is often chosen, though some opt for more creative interpretations, such as incorporating elements like feathers, birds, or stars into the design to reinforce the idea of hope and desire.

Strength

"Strength" tattoos are for those who wish to commemorate their capability and fortitude. This impactful word symbolizes physical strength, emotional endurance, and bravery, perfectly capturing the essence of someone's determination to confront provocation with boldness. For many, it is a bold testament to personal empowerment and survival, signifying their effectiveness. The concept of strength is multifaceted; it encompasses the idea of overcoming battles, whether they be physical or emotional. A "Strength" tattoo reflects this journey, showcasing an individual's true character and commitment to prosperity. Both "Hope" and "Strength" act as enduring symbols that inspire the wearer to conquer one's weaknesses and champion their narrative of progress and optimism. These tattoos can mark grand moments in a person's life.

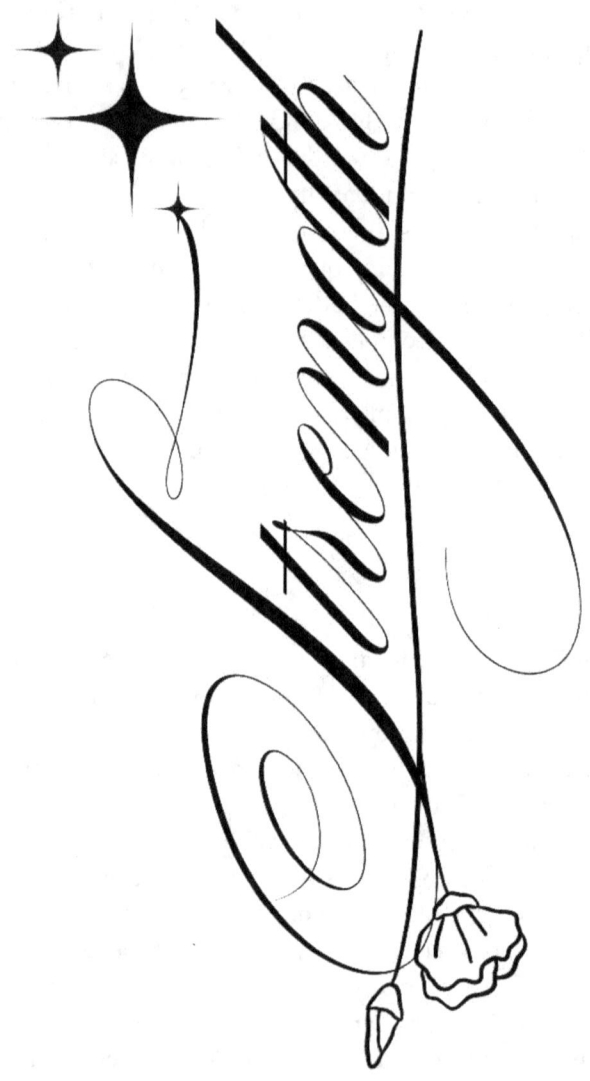

A single word 'Strength' design

Courage

The word "Courage" goes beyond mere bravery; it embodies the core ability to confront fear and take decisive action despite uncertainty. Engraving a "Courage" tattoo on your skin can mark a transformative moment in your life—perhaps a time when you defied your doubts or embraced the unknown. Embracing courage means recognizing that fear is a natural part of life, but it doesn't have to dictate your actions. It represents fortitude, strength, and the relentless pursuit of your goals. When you wear a symbol of courage, you carry the essence of bravery and the strength to inspire yourself and others around you. Moreover, a courage tattoo can also honor the spirit of those who have shown phenomenal bravery in their lives, reminding one of the struggles faced by individuals and communities striving for justice and equality. By choosing this ink, you align yourself with a legacy of potential and inspire a culture of empowerment. A courage tattoo is not merely an image; it's an explanation of intent to live life fully, fearlessly, and passionately.

Freedom

Freedom symbolizing autonomy and liberation from constraints that bind us. A "Freedom" tattoo encapsulates the essence of breaking through personal barriers, achieving progress, and celebrating authenticity. Wearing a representation of freedom is not just an expression but an enduring symbol to pursue a life released by limitations, propelling you toward your true potential. It inspires action and motivates the wearer and those who see it to live freely and peacefully. Ultimately, a freedom tattoo is more than an aesthetic choice; it's a powerful acknowledgment of your commitment to a free life, free choices, and desires, encouraging you to navigate your path freely with courage and authenticity.

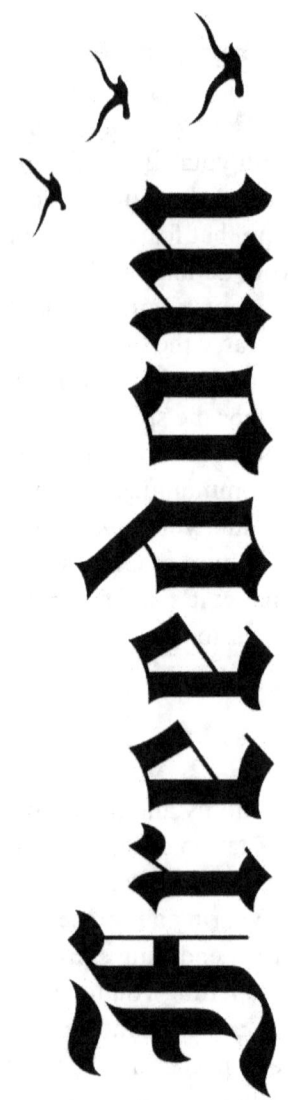

A single word 'freedom' design

Quotes: Personal Philosophies, Motivational Phrases

Quotes hold a unique place in tattoo art, allowing individuals to ink words that resemble their core beliefs, life experiences, or worldviews. A favorite quote can provide guidance, act as a daily affirmation, or mark a significant moment in one's life. These tattoos are often chosen after careful thought, reflecting values and philosophies the wearer holds dear.

Personal Philosophies

Many people choose quotes that reflect their personal philosophies or life mottos. These could be phrases from famous authors, thinkers, or simply lines that have been inspiring. Popular examples include:

"This too shall pass" – A reminder that difficult times are temporary.

"It is what it is" – An expression of tolerance and acceptance of difficult times.

Motivational Phrases

Motivational quotes are a frequent choice for tattoos, offering daily encouragement to push through difficulty or to stay focused on one's goals. Examples include:

"Believe in yourself" – A simple yet powerful reminder of self-confidence.

"Never give up" – A tattoo that pushes the wearer to persevere.

"Dream big" – Encourages the wearer to aim high and chase their ambitions.

"Stay strong" – A motivational phrase to motivate oneself to keep strong.

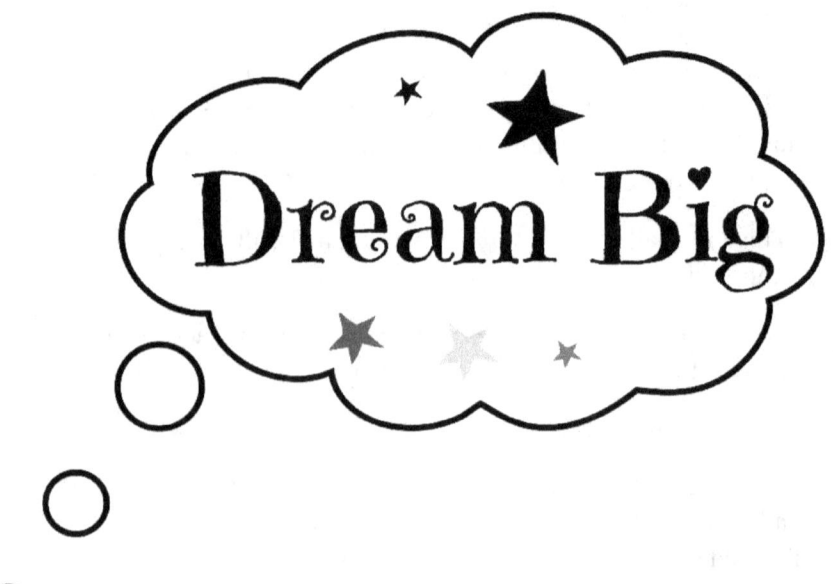

A simple 'dream big' phrase design

Names and Dates: Commemorations, Tribute Tattoos

Tattoos featuring names and dates are often completely personal, displaying tributes to loved ones, special moments, or important events. These tattoos can commemorate relationships, memorialize someone who has passed away, or momentous milestones. They carry strong emotional meaning and are often chosen to keep memories close.

Names

Name tattoos are one of the most intimate forms of tattooing. People often choose to tattoo the names of loved ones, such as parents, children, or significant others, as a symbol of eternal love and connection. The name of a child is a particularly common choice, signifying the deep bond between parent and child.

Dates

Dates are frequently tattooed to commemorate memorable life events, such as the birth of a child, the date of a wedding, or the anniversary of a loved one's passing. Roman Numerals are often used in date tattoos.

Chapter Conclusion

Inspirational words and phrases in tattoos encapsulate the essence of one's beliefs and ideas. From single words like hope, strength, courage, and freedom to profound quotes, names, and dates, each tattoo provides a testament to a unique narrative.

Custom scripts and calligraphy further enhance the emotional impact, allowing individuals to infuse their tattoos with personal style and creativity. These tattoos become more than mere ink on skin; they transform into powerful symbols of identity. Through the artistry of words, tattoos become lasting artworks of what truly matters.

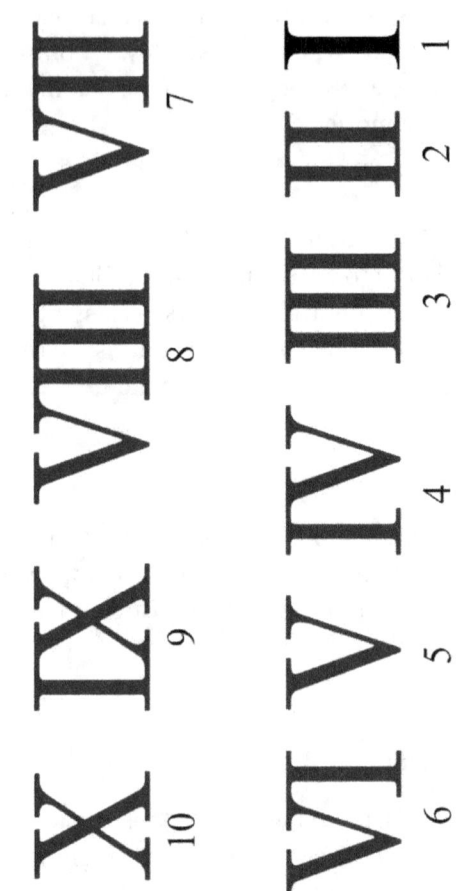

Roman Numerals from 1 to 10

116

Chapter 8: Modern and Minimalist Tattoos

Modern and minimalist tattoos have carved a distinct niche in the ever-evolving world of tattoo art. Characterized by their clean lines, simplicity, and understated elegance, these often embracing themes of nature and geometry. This style has gained popularity for its ability to portray a variety of meanings without overwhelming imagery, making each piece a thoughtful statement on skin.

Modern and minimalist tattoos represent a shift in the tattoo world, where less is more. These designs focus on simplicity, subtlety, and elegance while still conveying thoughtful meanings. They are often favored by those who want their tattoos to blend seamlessly into their everyday lives, providing a meaningful connection without being overly bold or intricate.

Minimalist tattoos have gained popularity in recent years for their simple shapes and designs. Whether it's through the use of fine lines, dot work, or minimalist symbols, these tattoos allow wearers to express themselves in a refined and understated manner.

In this chapter, we will explore different aspects of modern minimalist tattoos, including their design philosophies, symbolism, and the unique artistic techniques that bring these simple yet impactful tattoos to life.

Minimalist Designs: Simplicity, Subtlety, Elegance

Minimalist designs are known for their simplicity and clean lines. They focus on reducing a concept to its most essential form while still capturing its core meaning. Rather than relying on complex details and shading, minimalist tattoos use basic lines and symbols to portray different messages.

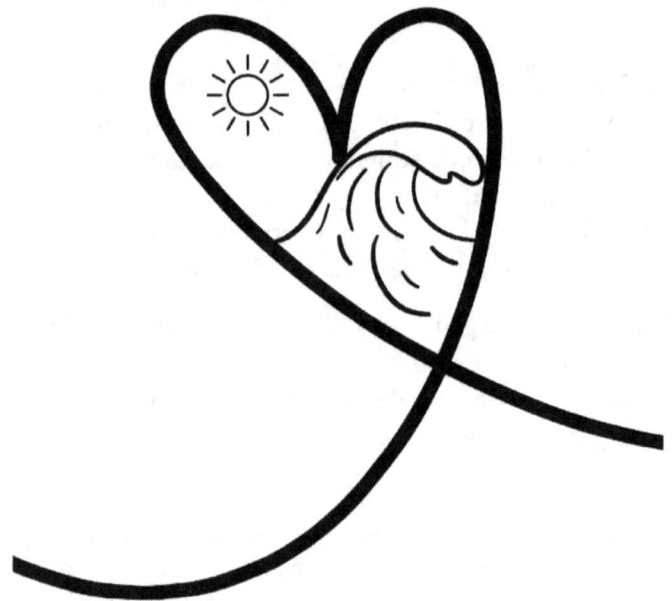

A simple heart design

Simplicity

Minimalist tattoos thrive on simplicity. A small, clean design can hold as much meaning as a large, intricate piece. The idea is to distill a concept down to its purest form, allowing the tattoo to speak for itself without the distraction of excess detail. This simplicity is often appealing to those who prefer a more subtle, delicate look, making their tattoos a part of their overall aesthetic rather than a standout feature.

Examples of Simple Designs: A minimalist mountain range to symbolize adventure or perseverance, a single wave to represent the conservation and flow, or a small heart to signify love in its most basic form.

Subtlety

Subtle tattoos can have strong meanings without needing to be the focal point. Minimalist designs are often small and placed in inconspicuous locations, allowing them to remain private. This subtlety appeals to those who want their tattoos to be a quiet indication of important values and moments without drawing too much attention. Small tattoo designs on the wrist or on the ankle are common for minimalist designs.

Elegance

Elegance is a key aspect of minimalist tattoos. The simplicity of the design, combined with the precise lines and thoughtful placement, results in an overall sense of sophistication. Minimalist tattoos often have a refined, delicate quality that adds to their visual appeal. Minimalist designs often rely on negative space and balance to create an elegant composition. A single line or small shape can feel graceful and intentional when placed thoughtfully on the body, giving the tattoo a sense of timelessness.

An example of a simple mountain, sun, river design

Line Tattoos: Tenacity, Continuity, and Clarity

Line tattoos epitomize the essence of minimalist tattoo art. These designs utilize clean, unbroken lines to create forms and represent meanings without relying on shading or intricate patterns. Their versatility enables artists to craft everything from geometric designs to abstract shapes, animals, and portraits— each brought to life through meticulously placed lines.

Tenacity

In the realm of minimalist tattooing, the true significance often lies in the simplicity of the design. Line tattoos project their power through straightforwardness, stripping away unnecessary details to emphasize the core components of the design. For instance, a single vertical line might convey stability and structure, while a gently curved line could symbolize fluidity. An arrow, depicted with just a few essential lines, can signify direction, intention, or determination in one's adventure.

Continuity

One of the most profound symbols within line tattoos is that of continuity and ongoing flow. The seamless nature of the lines can depict a continuous endeavour. This concept is particularly emphasized in designs such as mandalas and geometric shapes, where each line contributes to a larger, cohesive narrative. Many line tattoos embrace abstraction, using continuous or intersecting lines to evoke depth and meaning. A design that loops back on itself can signify cycles of life, while parallel lines may represent the choices or paths we navigate, illustrating the interconnectedness of our experiences.

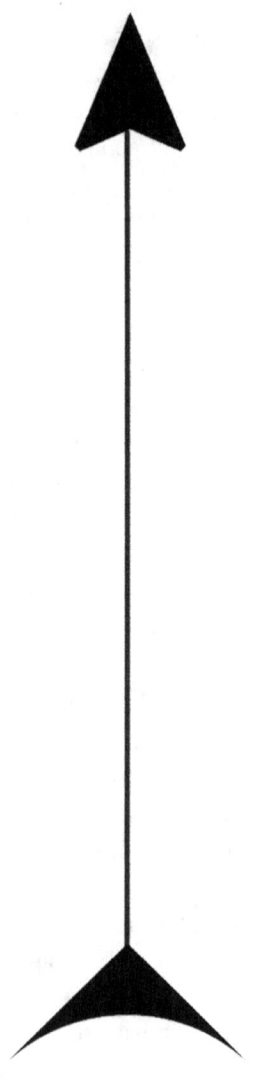

A simple arrow line design

Clarity

The clarity found in line tattoos is among their most compelling attributes. Freed from the distractions of shading or color, these tattoos offer a clear and direct visual message. This simplicity allows the design to communicate its meaning effectively and immediately. Minimalistic representations of animals, celestial motifs, and even landscapes are often crafted with just a handful of clean lines, resulting in visually appealing and uncomplicated designs. Additionally, line tattoos lend themselves well to abstract art, inviting one's interpretation while retaining a sense of clarity.

Dot Work: Patience, Progress, Precision

Dot work tattoos, also known as stippling, are created using a series of small dots that form larger images or patterns. While minimalist in nature, dot work requires immense patience and precision, both from the tattoo artist and the wearer. These tattoos can range from delicate, single-point designs to more intricate geometric or abstract patterns.

Patience

Dot work tattoos take time. The process of building an image or design out of thousands of tiny dots requires patience as designs can take many hours to complete. Each dot contributes to the final design, and the result is a tattoo that can carry a sense of calm, diligence, and care. The gradual buildup of dots to create shading or texture is different from the standard techniques used in tattoo art, but can have some beautiful designs and striking effects.

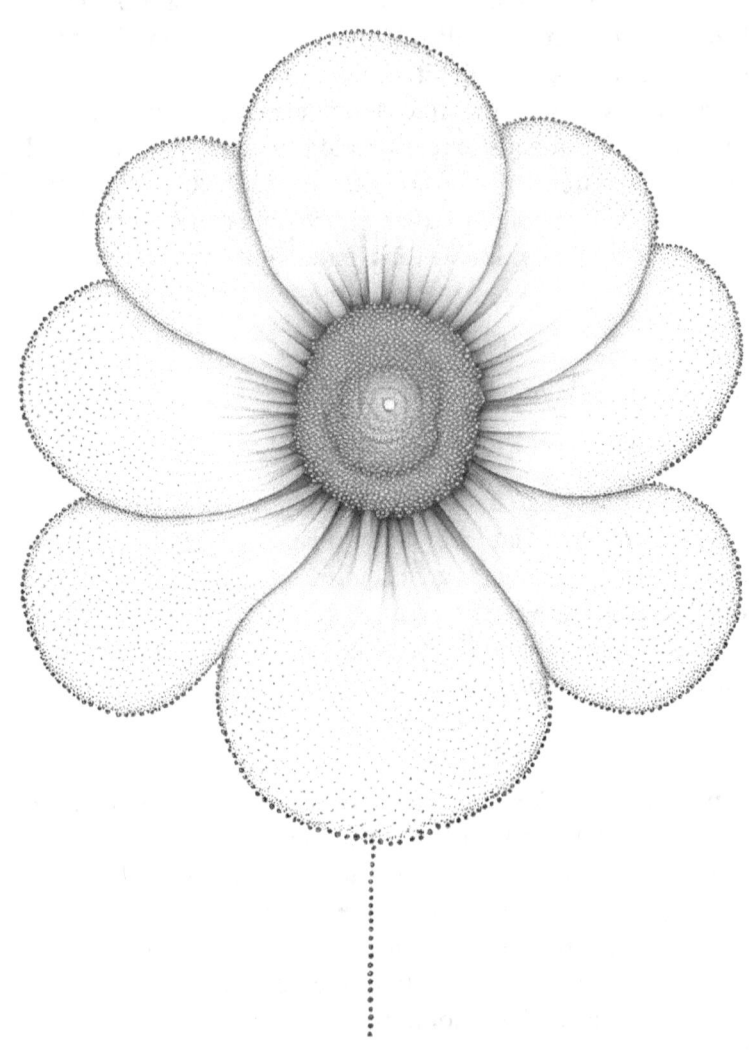

A simple dot work flower tattoo design

Small Tattoos: A Moment Captured, Personal Achievements

Minimalist tattoos have emerged as a significant trend within contemporary body art. Their charm lies in their understated elegance, effectively encapsulating specific memories.

Capturing Moments

Minimalist tattoos often encapsulate pivotal milestones in one's life. Be it the arrival of a new family member, a hard-fought achievement, or a remarkable milestone. For instance, a tiny airplane might signify a love for adventure, a subtle paddle could represent a passion for water sports, or a delicate star might celebrate a dream realized. Though these designs often boast minimalistic details, they allow wearers to carry treasured memories wherever they go.

Celebrating Personal Achievements

Additionally, small tattoos are frequently selected to commemorate personal achievements, such as reaching long-awaited goals. Each piece serves as a distinct acknowledgment of both small victories and monumental progress, enhancing the overall impact of these milestones. The modern embrace of minimalist designs has led to a surge in their popularity as a powerful medium for self-expression. These tattoos embody grace and simplicity, enabling individuals to share their unique narratives and emotions without overwhelming complexity. Their meanings often reflect core values or life experiences, transforming them into treasured meaningful symbols.

Chapter Conclusion

Through clean lines, understated symbols, and compact designs, these tattoos capture meaning in a way that feels both timeless and refined. Whether it's a single line representing continuity, a series of dots symbolizing progress, or a small symbol marking a personal milestone, minimalist tattoos offer a small yet impactful way to carry meaningful messages with you.

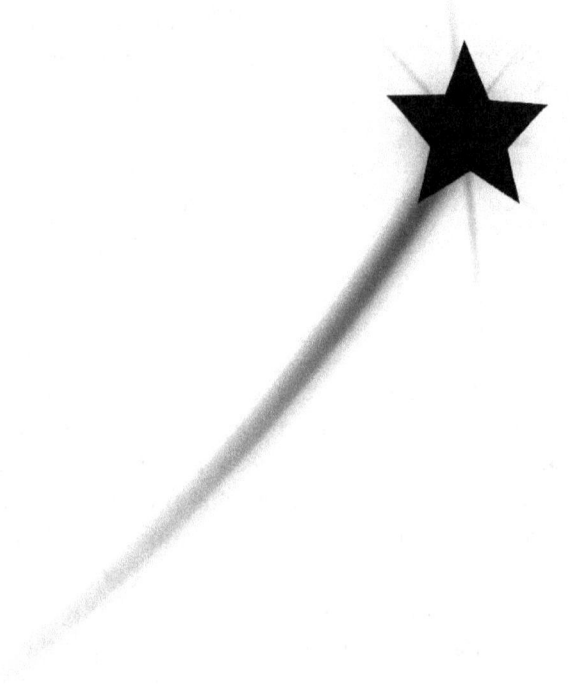

A simple shooting star design

Chapter 9: Surreal Tattoos

Surreal tattoos inhabit a captivating realm where reality intertwines with imagination, inviting visual art to explore the intricate depths of the human psyche. Unfettered by the constraints of logic or ordinary existence, they draw vibrant inspiration from dreams, fantasies, and the enigmatic unconscious. This form of surrealism in tattoos encourages viewers to explore peculiar juxtapositions, surprising connections, and profound symbolism. Each piece often visually explores complex emotions, thought-provoking ideas, and concepts. In this chapter, we'll delve deep into the enchanting world of surreal tattoos, unraveling the meanings behind fragmented images, dream-like elements, abstract forms, and the striking interplay between geometric precision and fluid designs. Surreal tattoos display otherworldly body art, empowering wearers to tap into their subconscious and translate their innermost thoughts and feelings.

Fragmented Images: Complex Emotions and Inner Conflict

One of the most expressive characteristics of surreal tattoos is the use of fragmented or disjointed imagery to show one's internal feelings and emotions. These designs often deconstruct a recognizable figure or symbol, reassembling it in astonishingly unexpected ways. This fragmentation can powerfully represent the turmoil of intense emotions like love, loss, fear, or success. For example, a surreal portrait may be disassembled into several floating, ethereal parts, symbolizing a person's view of their identity or the sensation of being pulled in myriad directions. Similarly, a fractured heart could encapsulate emotional chaos, the experience of heartache, or the complexities of love. By breaking down an image into smaller, seemingly disconnected elements, these tattoos suggest that emotions and individual experiences are rarely straightforward—they are layered, beautiful, messy, and extraordinarily multifaceted. Through such artistry, wearers express not only their complexities but also their unique narratives.

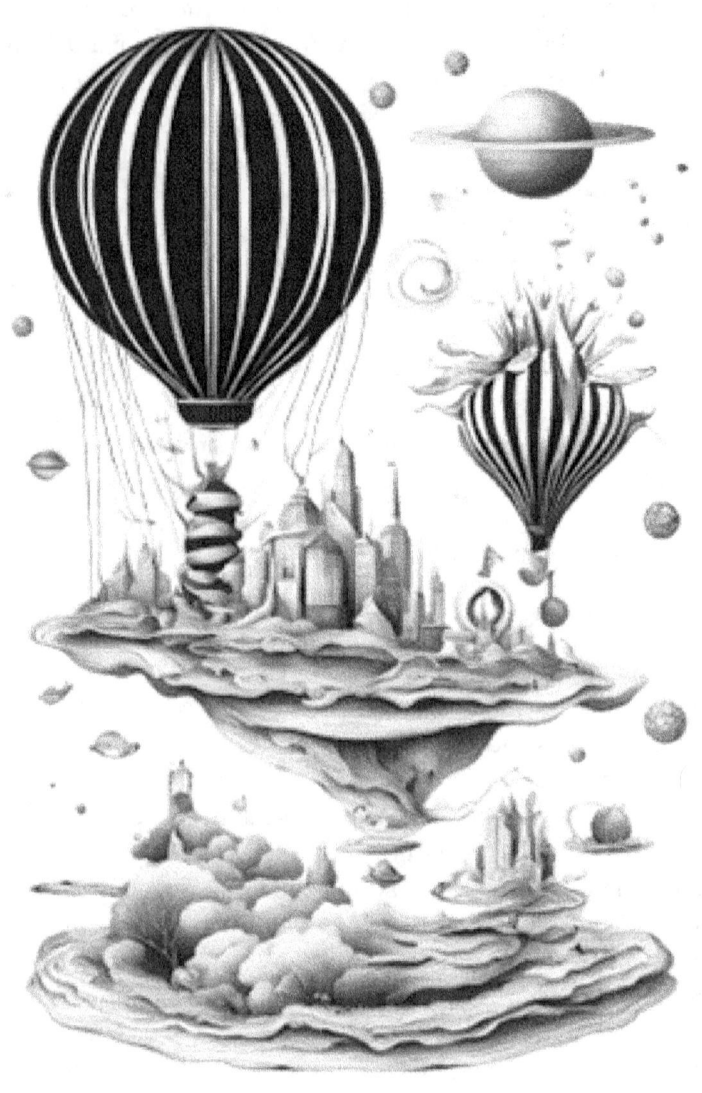

A tattoo design of a surreal floating world

Surreal Elements: Dreams, Imagination, and the Unconscious Mind

Surreal tattoos are heavily influenced by dream-like imagery and the world of the subconscious. These designs often evoke feelings of mystery, wonder, and intrigue, drawing from the irrational and the fantastical. The dream world is a place where the impossible becomes possible, where reality is fluid, and where hidden desires and fears come to the surface. In surreal tattoos, you might find elements like floating objects, distorted landscapes, or animals in unexpected contexts. For example, a tree growing out of a person's head could symbolize wisdom or the flourishing of new ideas. A clock with melting hands might represent the fluid nature of time and our perception of it, exploring possible anxieties about aging or our relationship with the past and future.

These surreal elements often come together to create a scene that feels like it was pulled straight from a dream—or a nightmare. They offer a way for the wearer to explore their imagination and express feelings or ideas that are difficult to articulate in a literal sense. By using surreal imagery, these tattoos give life to the intangible, allowing the wearer to explore concepts like fear, joy, uncertainty, or desire in a deeply personal and symbolic way. Moreover, surreal tattoos offer a canvas for storytelling, inviting viewers to interpret the imagery based on their own perspectives. This makes each tattoo unique, rich with meaning, and vastly connected to the wearer's life story, further enhancing its emotional depth and artistic allure. Dream-like tattoos represent unusual forms of personal expression and invite curiosity and conversation. Each design sparks the imagination, transforming skin into a canvas that reflects the wearer's thoughts, goals, and dreams, ultimately creating a lasting connection with those who see them.

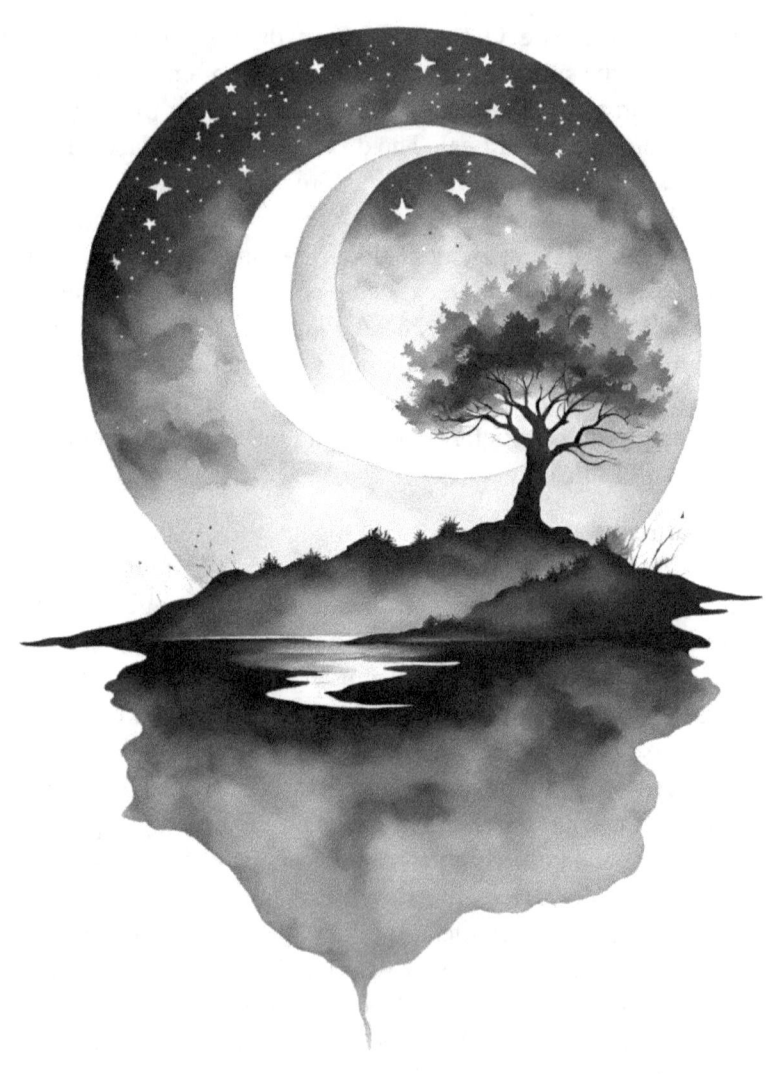

A surreal and dreamy landscape tattoo design

Abstract Forms: Personal Interpretations and Unique Symbols

One of the key features of surrealism is its departure from literal representations. Surreal tattoos often feature abstract forms, which allow for open interpretation and invite the viewer to project their own meanings onto the design. These abstract shapes and lines can exhibit meanings or ideas that go beyond what can be easily explained.

For instance, a series of geometric shapes seamlessly melting into one another could suggest the merging of different aspects of a person's multifaceted personality or the blending of past and present experiences. What makes abstract surreal tattoos so compelling is their extraordinary ability to carry deeply unique meanings without being tied to any specific, recognizable imagery. They encourage a more emotional and introspective response, allowing both the wearer and the viewer to derive their own translation from the piece. This makes abstract surreal tattoos an ideal choice for those who want their tattoos to stand as a fluid source of meaning and reflection rather than a fixed symbol with a singular interpretation.

Juxtaposition of Real and Imagined: The Play of Reality and Fantasy

Surreal tattoos often combine elements of the real world with those of the imagined, creating a striking contrast that questions our perceptions. This juxtaposition is a hallmark of surrealism, blurring the lines between what we see and what we imagine. It invites the viewer to explore the boundary between the possible and the impossible. For example, a tattoo might feature a hyper-realistic eye surrounded by abstract swirls and shapes, creating a blend of the familiar and the fantastical. This could symbolize a person's ability to see beyond the surface or suggest the idea of perceiving the world in a different way. The combination of realism and surrealism allows the tattoo to play with ideas of perception, reality, and imagination.

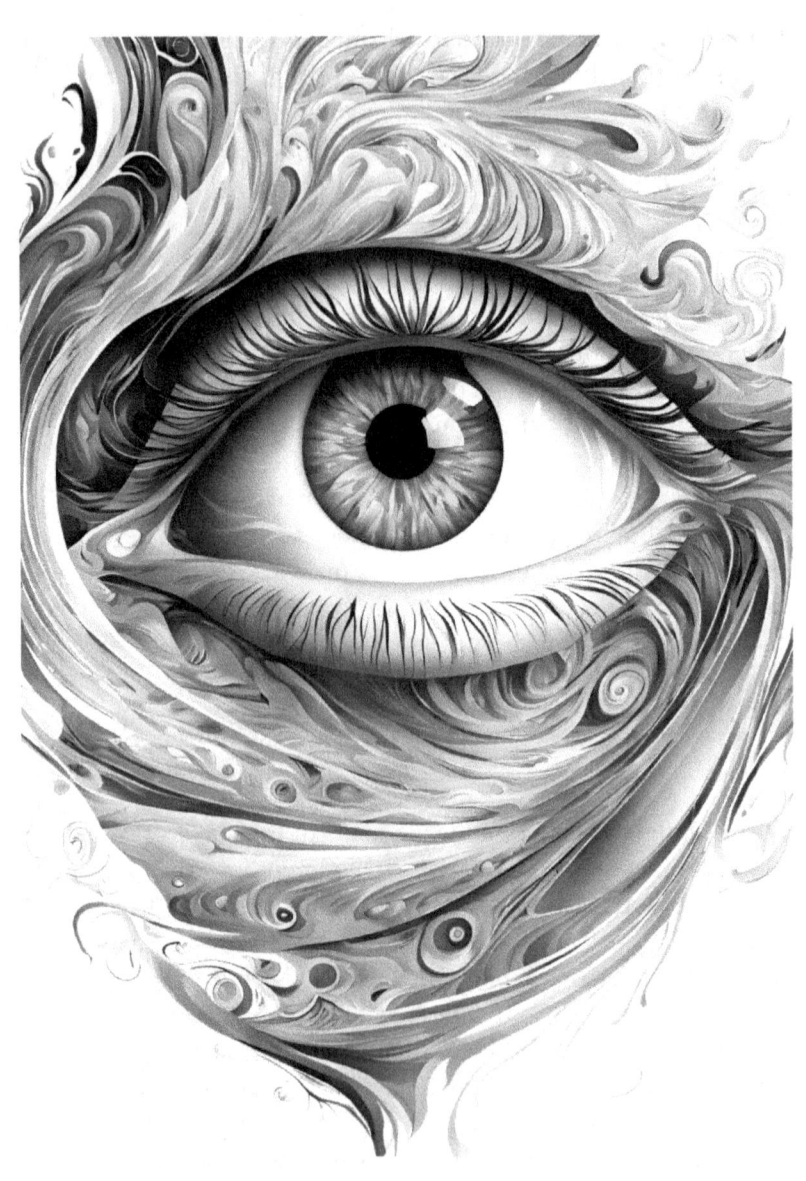

A surreal eye tattoo surrounded by a swirl design

The interplay of reality and fantasy in surreal tattoos often results in a visually striking and thought-provoking designs. These tattoos ask us to question what we know to be true and open ourselves up to new ways of thinking and interpreting the world.

Surrealism as a Journey of Self-Exploration

At its core, surrealism is about exploring the depths of the human psyche, the unconscious mind, and the realm of dreams and fantasies. Surreal tattoos offer a unique way for individuals to explore these inner worlds, using art as a means of discovery. Each surreal tattoo is like a puzzle or a dream—a collection of symbols, images, and shapes that may not make immediate sense but hold deep meaning for the wearer.

What makes surreal tattoos particularly astonishing is their ability to communicate ideas that are difficult to put into words. They allow individuals to express their inner thoughts in a visual form that is both personal and universal. The abstract nature of surrealism invites introspection, encouraging both the wearer and the viewer to find their own meanings within the design.

In many ways, surreal tattoos are a exploration into the unknown—an exploration of the self, the mind, and the world of imagination. They are an invitation to step beyond the boundaries of reality and enter a space where anything is possible, where logic could be suspended, and where meaning can be found in the most unexpected places.

Chapter Conclusion

Surreal tattoos give wearers the freedom to express the complexity of their underlying feelings, using fragmented images, dreamy elements, abstract forms, and the blending of reality and imagination to tell a story. For those who want a tattoo that goes beyond the ordinary, surreal tattoos offer a rich and versatile option. They allow for endless creativity and interpretation, making them perfect for anyone looking to express ideas that are difficult to capture with more traditional designs.

Chapter 10: Technological and Futuristic Tattoos

As technology continues to shape our world, it also influences the art of tattooing. Technological and futuristic tattoos are an exciting category that merges traditional tattoo artistry with modern themes and advanced techniques. This chapter explores the various aspects of technological and futuristic tattoos, including their inspiration, design elements, and the cultural significance they hold for those who choose them.

The Inspiration Behind Technological and Futuristic Tattoos

Technological and futuristic tattoos draw inspiration from a variety of sources, including science fiction, cyberpunk aesthetics, mechanics, and advancements in technology. These tattoos often incorporate elements that reflect a fascination with the future, the digital age, and the blending of human and machine.

Science fiction has long been a rich source of inspiration for futuristic tattoo designs. Iconic imagery from movies, books, and video games often finds its way into tattoo art. Themes such as space exploration, advanced robotics, and dystopian societies are commonly represented, capturing the imagination and wonder of what the future may hold.

Cyberpunk aesthetics, with their emphasis on high-tech, provide a gritty and visually striking style for tattoos. Elements such as circuit boards, neon lights, and biomechanical components are frequently used to create a look that is both edgy and sophisticated. These tattoos often reflect a commentary on the relationship between technology and society.

Advancements in technology also inspire tattoos that incorporate modern devices and digital symbols. From QR codes to barcodes, these designs capture the essence of our increasingly connected world. They act as a representation of how technology has become an integral part of our daily lives and our identity.

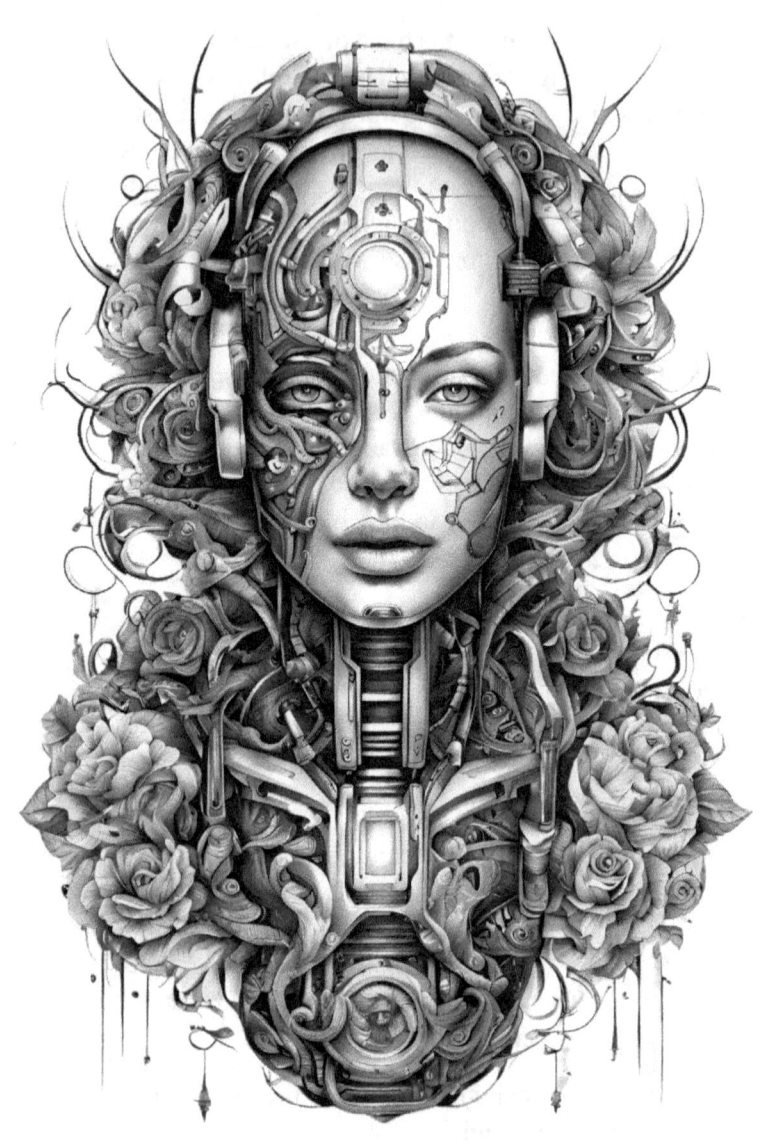

A robotic tattoo design

Design Elements of Technological and Futuristic Tattoos

The design elements of technological and futuristic tattoos are diverse and varied, reflecting the wide range of themes and inspirations within this category. Some common elements include:

1. Circuitry and Digital Patterns

One of the most recognizable design elements in technological tattoos is the use of circuitry and digital patterns. These designs mimic the intricate pathways found on circuit boards and electronic devices, creating a visually complex and detailed tattoo. Circuitry tattoos often symbolize intelligence and the integration of technology into human life.

Digital patterns, such as binary code or pixelated images, are also popular in futuristic tattoos. These designs can represent the digital age, information, and the idea of data as a form of expression. For example, a tattoo of binary code spelling out a meaningful word or phrase can be a unique way to combine a technological aesthetic.

2. Biomechanical Designs

Biomechanical tattoos are a distinctive style that blends organic and mechanical elements to create the illusion of machinery beneath the skin. These tattoos often feature realistic depictions of gears, pistons, and other mechanical components intertwined with human anatomy. The result is a striking and often surreal visual effect that explores the fusion of human and machine.

Biomechanical designs can symbolize the integration of technology into the human body, reflecting themes of enhancement, evolution, and the future of human capability. They also offer a highly customizable approach to tattooing, allowing for a wide range of interpretations and artistic designs.

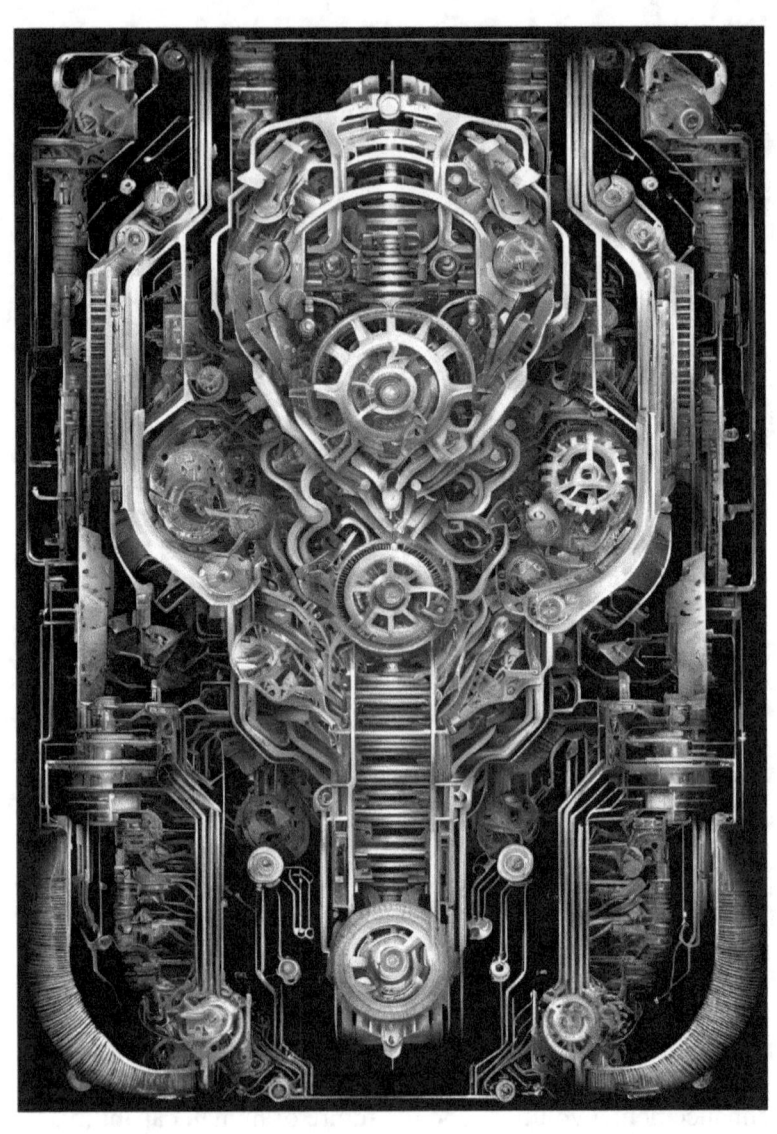

A futuristic mechanical design

3. Futuristic Landscapes and Imagery

Futuristic tattoos can include landscapes and imagery that depict stunning visions of the future. These designs can range from sprawling cityscapes featuring towering skyscrapers and flying vehicles to scenes of outer space showcasing distant planets and swirling galaxies. Using vibrant colors, intricate details, and dynamic shading helps bring these visions to life, creating a sense of wonder and excitement. These tattoos can symbolize a fascination with the unknown, representing the endless possibilities that lie ahead. They may also reflect personal aspirations for adventure, new discoveries, and a desire to push the boundaries of technological goals. As such, these designs often resonate with those who embrace innovation and seek to explore the uncharted territories of the human experience.

4. Abstract and Conceptual Designs

Technological and futuristic tattoos frequently push the boundaries of traditional tattoo artistry by incorporating abstract and conceptual designs. These tattoos may utilize geometric shapes, optical illusions, and unconventional patterns to create a contemporary and modern futuristic appearance. The emphasis is firmly placed on innovation and creativity, resulting in visually stimulating and thought-provoking tattoos. Abstract designs can represent many meanings, from the complexities and intricacies of the digital age to the ever-evolving nature of technology itself. They offer a distinctive avenue for individuals to express their thoughts, experiences, and feelings about the future and the role of technology. Such tattoos invite viewers to engage with them on multiple levels, prompting reflection and discussion about the future and how technology could shape our world.

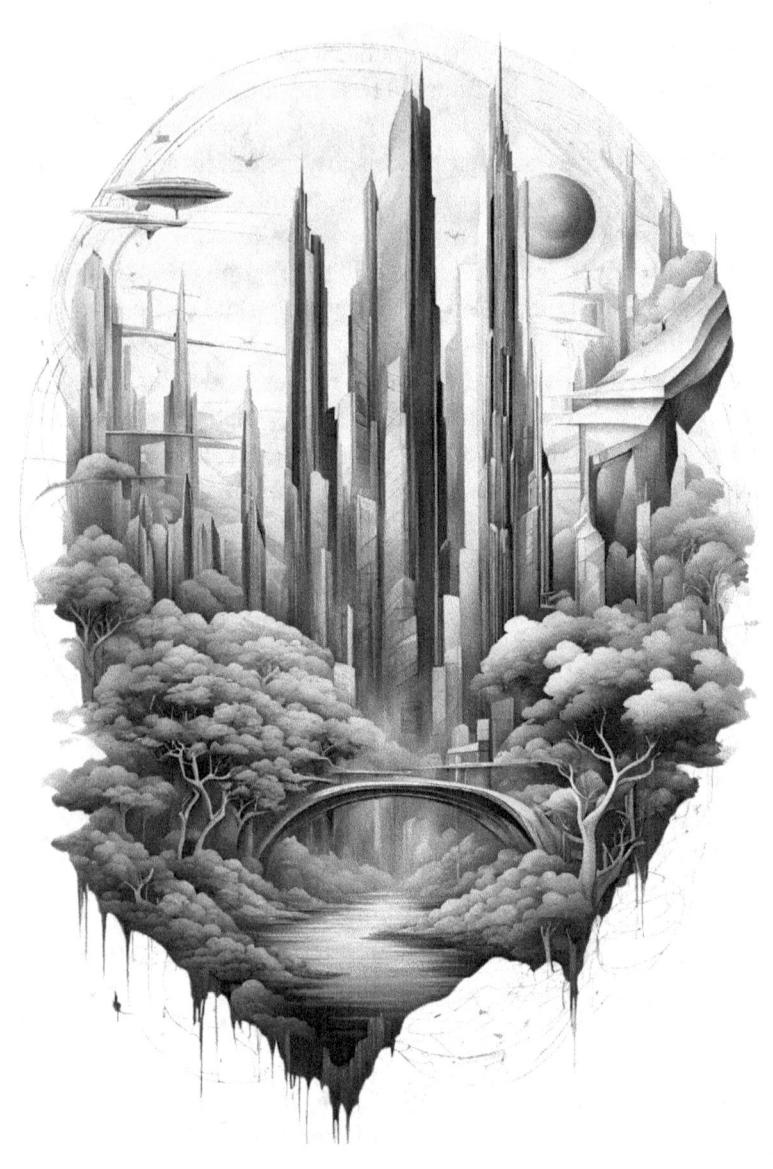

A futuristic landscape tattoo design

The Future of Technological and Futuristic Tattoos

As technology continues to advance, the possibilities for technological and futuristic tattoos are likely to expand. Innovations in tattooing techniques, such as the development of electronic tattoos, offer exciting new opportunities for integrating technology with body art.

The rise of augmented reality and virtual reality also holds potential for the future of tattooing. Imagine a tattoo that can be brought to life through augmented reality, revealing hidden designs, animations, or interactive elements when viewed through a smartphone or VR glasses. This technology could transform the way we experience and interact with tattoos, adding a new layer of depth and engagement.

In addition to technological advancements, the cultural landscape will continue to influence the evolution of futuristic tattoos. As society grapples with the implications of new technologies, these tattoos will likely reflect the ongoing dialogue about the role of technology in our lives.

Chapter Conclusion

Technological and futuristic tattoos represent an exciting intersection of traditional tattoo artistry and modern innovation. Drawing inspiration from science fiction and advancements in technology, these tattoos offer a unique way to explore themes of progress, identity, and the future.

As we look to the future, the possibilities for technological and futuristic tattoos are limitless. With continued advancements in technology and tattooing techniques, we can expect to see even more innovative and groundbreaking designs. These tattoos will not only continue to captivate and inspire but also provoke thought and discussion about the role of technology in shaping our world and our identity.

Final Thoughts: The Power of Tattoos and Their Meanings

Tattoos are creative ways to express oneself, symbols that narrate stories and resemble emotions in a visually captivating manner. Throughout this book, we've examined many tattoo motifs, styles, and interpretations, exploring their meanings and emotional interpretations. Whether it's a minimalist mark or a detailed depiction, every tattoo carries a meaning distinct to its wearer, reflecting life experiences, values, and memories. In exploring tattoo symbolism, we uncover how these designs mirror our personalities, and communicate with the world. Individuals can create a narrative that adapts over time by selecting specific motifs, capturing moments, memories, and emotions in a manner few other forms of art can.

From the earliest chapters, we examined nature-inspired tattoos, which draw ideas from the natural world and the emotions it invokes. Designs like flowers, trees, and animals are rich with meaning, often representing perseverance, transformation, and freedom. Each flower, from the delicate cherry blossom to the elegant dandelion, tells a tale of beauty, transience, and change.

Similarly, animal tattoos—featuring a fierce lion or a solitary wolf—explore our basic instincts and traits we aspire to embody. Nature-themed tattoos remind us of our bond with the environment. They represent natural attributes we wish to incorporate into our lives, making them creative symbols of courage and transformation. Choosing a nature-inspired tattoo allows individuals to express their admiration for the natural world while emphasizing the parallels between nature's cycles and unique experiences.

Geometric and minimalist tattoos distill symbolism into a refined and elegant form. These tattoos can portray intricate ideas about stability, unity, and development through basic shapes like circles, triangles, and lines. Each lline and shape can be intentional, allowing the design to carry significant meaning without needing elaborate details.

Conversely, abstract designs transport us into meanings and interpretations that elude simple explanations. By merging geometric shapes with fluid forms, abstract tattoos create a dynamic interplay between order and chaos, structure and freedom. This style, often associated with contemporary art, is a unique platform for exhibiting ideas such as internal conflict and the complexities of the human experience. Abstract tattoos are visually captivating and encourage viewers to delve deeper to uncover layers of meaning.

Tattoos inspired by celestial and elemental themes represent something universal and timeless. The sun, moon, stars, and planets have guided and inspired humanity for centuries, each carrying a wealth of meanings: the sun symbolizes vitality, the moon embodies mystery and change, while stars signify dreams and navigation. Planetary tattoos reflect the quest for discovery and exploration, illustrating the desire for expansion and insight. Elemental tattoos—representing fire, water, air, and earth— invoke the fundamental forces of nature and the qualities they embody. Fire-themed designs express transformation and passion, while water symbolizes adaptability and emotional depth. Air contrasts with the grounded nature of earth, embodying freedom. These tattoo ideas can reflect the natural world's influence on human life and psyche, connecting tattoo wearers to their feelings and the broader universe.

Tattoos featuring mythical creatures delve into realms of fantasy and folklore, embodying traits that transcend the natural world. These legendary beings carry profound symbolism, from dragons and phoenixes to unicorns and griffins. A dragon tattoo might signify protection or wisdom, while a phoenix represents renewal and rebirth. Each mythical creature possesses unique attributes, allowing the wearer to connect with ideals that resonate deeply with their experiences. These designs offer not just visual appeal; they channel the qualities and myths represented by these creatures. They provide a means for individuals to project their courage, adventurous spirit, and individuality.

The number of meanings within tattoo body art is incredibly diverse, representing a wide array of personal experiences, cultural heritages, and artistic visions. Tattoos can embody emotions like affection, grief, fortitude, or core values, acting as distinct signs of beliefs and identity. Each artwork tells a particular and unique story to the individual who wears it.

Thank you for choosing this book! I hope you've discovered some fascinating insights into the meanings of tattoos and the stories that accompany them. Enjoy exploring this captivating art form!

Glossary of Tattoo Meanings

Rose – Love, Passion, Sacrifice

Lotus – Purity, Overcoming Obstacles

Cherry Blossom – Transience, Beauty, Life's Fragility

Dandelion – Hope, New Beginnings

Sunflower – Happiness, Vitality, Positivity

Tiger – Strength, Courage, Power

Lion – Leadership, Bravery, Royalty

Wolf – Loyalty, Family, Independence

Elephant – Wisdom, Strength, Patience

Bear – Protection, Courage, Grounding

Owl – Knowledge, Wisdom, Mystery

Eagle – Freedom, Vision, Power

Hawk – Clarity, Focus, Strength

Snake – Wisdom, Rebirth, Protection

Butterfly – Transformation, Beauty, New Beginnings

Dragon – Power, Protection, Wisdom

Phoenix – Rebirth, Immortality, Renewal

Koi Fish – Perseverance, Strength, Determination

Anchor – Stability, Strength, Safety

Feather – Freedom, Lightness, Spirituality

Tree – Growth, Stability, Strength

Mountain – Endurance, Strength, Goals

Ocean – Calmness, Depth, Power

Wave – Change, Love the sea, Motion

Moon – Femininity, Intuition, Change

Sun – Vitality, Energy, Power

Stars – Guidance, Ambition, Dreams

Constellation – Fate, Cosmic Connection, Destiny

Planet – Discovery, Mystery, Exploration

Lightning – Sudden Change, Power, Inspiration

Fire – Passion, Anger, Energy

Water – Purification, Emotional Depth, Adaptability

Air – Freedom, Intelligence, Communication

Galaxy – Infinity, Exploration, The Unknown

Comet – Rare Moments, Significant Events

Yin and Yang – Balance, Duality, Harmony

Hourglass – Time, Mortality, Impermanence

Infinity Symbol – Eternity, Limitless Possibilities

Mandalas – Balance, Inner Peace, Spirituality

Triangle – Stability, Change, Creativity

Circle – Wholeness, Unity, Eternity

Dot Work – Precision, Progress, Focus

Line Tattoo – Simplicity, Continuity, Clarity

Skull – Mortality, Memory of lost one's, Protection

Skeleton – Mortality, Life's Cycle, Strength

Heart – Love, Compassion, Courage

Eye – Vision, Protection, Intuition

Hand – Power, Creation, Connection

Portrait – Identity, Memory, Tribute

Chakras – Energy, Balance, Alignment

Unicorn – Purity, Innocence, Magic

Griffin – Courage, Honor, Protection

Fairy – Freedom, Innocence, Magic

Celtic Knot – Eternity, Interconnectedness, Life

Geometric Tattoo – Precision, Stability, Order

Surreal Tattoo – Dreams, Imagination

Fragmented Image – Inner Conflict, Complex Emotions

Abstract Symbols – Uniqueness, Freedom, Interpretation

Minimalist Tattoo – Simplicity, Elegance, Subtlety

Bird – Freedom, Aspiration, Vision

Butterfly – Transformation, Beauty

Snake and Dagger – Conflict, Power, Survival

Compass – Direction, Guidance, Purpose

Arrow – Focus, Strength, Moving Forward

Scorpion – Protection, Defense, Survival

Sword – Strength, Honor, Protection

Shield – Defense, Strength, Courage

Crown – Power, Royalty, Authority

Clock – Time, Life, Mortality

Key – Opportunity, Freedom, Secrets

Lock – Security, Protection, Secrets

Ship – Adventure, Journey, Exploration

Octopus – Intelligence, Adaptability, Mystery

Hummingbird – Joy, Resilience, Energy

Fox – Cunning, Intelligence, Adaptability

Dragonfly – Change, Transformation, Grace

Bumblebee – Hard Work, Community, Focus

Spider – Patience, Creativity, Connection

Paw Print – Loyalty, Companionship, Love for Animals

Turtle – Longevity, Patience

Shark – Strength, Confidence, Fierceness

Whale – Depth, Wisdom, Emotional Strength

Dolphin – Playfulness, Intelligence, Friendship

Lioness – Feminine Strength, Courage, Leadership

Peacock – Beauty, Pride, Confidence

Horseshoe – Luck, Protection, Fortune

Fireworks – Celebration, Joy, Moments of Importance

Phoenix Feather – Rebirth, Renewal, Strength

Broken Heart – Heartache, Loss, Recovery

Paper Airplane – Holidays, Travel, Simplicity

Balloon – Joy, Release, Lightness

Music Note – Passion, Art, Personal Expression

Puzzle Piece – Individuality, Uniqueness, Life's Complexity

Robot – Modernity, Logic, Evolution

Moon Phases – Life Cycles, Change, Personal improvement

Lighthouse – Guidance, Hope, Safety

Mermaid – Mystery, Femininity, Freedom

Chess Pieces – Strategy, Intelligence, Power Dynamics

Book – Knowledge, Learning, Personal Story

Image and Text Credits

The majority of this book's text and images have been meticulously created using advanced AI tools, showcasing the exciting potential and creativity of technology in today's literary landscape.